Good Preaching

# Why Expository Preaching?

David Jackman

PT RESOURCES

CHRISTIAN
**FOCUS**

Scripture quotations are from *The Holy Bible, English Standard Version*, copyright © 2001 by Crossway Bibles, a publishing ministry of Good News Publishers. Used by permission. All rights reserved. ESV Text Edition: 2011.

Scripture quotations marked 'NIV' are taken from the *HOLY BIBLE, NEW INTERNATIONAL VERSION* ®. NIV®. Copyright ©1973, 1978, 1984 by International Bible Society. Used by permission of Zondervan. All rights reserved.

Copyright © Proclamation Trust

paperback ISBN 978-1-5271-0385-6
epub ISBN 978-1-5271-0435-8
mobi ISBN 978-1-5271-0436-5

10 9 8 7 6 5 4 3 2 1

Published in 2019
by
Christian Focus Publications Ltd.,
Geanies House, Fearn, Ross-shire,
IV20 1TW, Great Britain
with
Proclamation Trust Resources,
Willcox House, 140-148 Borough High Street,
London, SE1 1LB, England, Great Britain.
www.proctrust.org.uk

www.christianfocus.com

Cover design by Tom Barnard

Printed in Malta

# CONTENTS

# Series Preface

In 1592, the Puritan William Perkins published a tract on preaching that he called 'The Art of Prophesying'. He recognised that 'the preparation of sermons is an everyday task in the church, but it is still a tremendous responsibility and by no means easy. In fact it is doubtful if there is a more difficult challenge in the theological disciplines than that of homiletics .'

Since its beginnings in the summer of 1981, the Proclamation Trust has been committed to helping preachers in that tremendous – and difficult – responsibility. We believe that the Bible is God's written word and that, by the work of the Holy Spirit, as it is faithfully preached, God's voice is truly heard. With Perkins, we are confident that through the preaching of the Word 'those who hear are called into the state of grace, and preserved in it'.

This series of short books is designed to help preachers in that 'everyday task'. Experienced practitioners share their wisdom, gained after years of 'toil, struggling with all his energy that he powerfully works within us' (Col. 1:28-29).

We hope that these short books will help all of us to progress in our understanding of the task in hand; to set the novice preacher on a course of faithful preaching; to hone the skills of the experienced preacher; to help preaching groups sharpen one another.

However you use this book we hope that it will achieve its twin aims. That you would <u>get</u> preaching (understanding the task at hand), and get <u>preaching</u> (doing more preaching). May God use these books to renew a commitment in all of us to preach the Word (2 Tim. 4:2).

Jon Gemmell & Nigel Styles
Series Editors

# 1
# UNDERSTANDING THE MOTIVATION

The preacher cut a very impressive figure. His voice was resonant, his appearance immaculate, his manner confident and assured. He told the gathering of ministers, who had come to the conference on expository preaching, that it was precisely on such a foundation that his own very large congregation had been built. He opened his Bible and read a brief passage. Then he closed it and filled the next thirty minutes with anecdotes and illustrations; entertaining and humorous, emotional and heart-rending — a stellar performance. But whatever it was, it was not exposition. And, sadly, his other colleagues, who had also come to 'model' Biblical exposition, did exactly the same.

What is expository preaching? Clearly it is more than simply using the Bible, or what is sometimes described as 'Bible-based ministry'. Many preachers use the Bible—often as a starting point, frequently for illustrative material—but that is not the same as expounding the Bible. The Bible text is used rather like a trampoline, to bounce off in all sorts of unpredictable directions. But the ultimate authority behind such preaching is inevitably the preacher himself, with his own particular interests or agenda.

On the other hand, expository preaching has come to be associated with a style of preaching more suited to the lecture hall than the church family. In dealing with the minutiae of the Biblical text the preacher becomes lost in a maze of exegetical rabbit-runs, so that the net effect is heavily academic, overly intellectual and generally fails to feed the flock. But that is not expository preaching either.

## Definition: Who's in the Driving-seat?

At its simplest, I would define expository preaching as preaching which takes the Bible seriously; so seriously that the Biblical text totally governs and directs the contents of the talk or sermon. Let me try to explain.

Think, for a moment, about your church, or your own preaching, under the analogy of a car, and ask yourself, 'Where is the Bible in the car?' Unhappily, there are too many churches where it lies buried in the boot, long forgotten and ignored. In others, it has progressed to the back seat, though as with many a back-seat driver, its function often seems to be to act as a distracting irritant to the driver at the wheel. However, the Bible's most common location, especially in evangelical churches, is in the passenger seat. Alongside the driver, it can act as a conversation partner, provide a useful map-reading service, a sort of celestial sat-nav to give directions, but sometimes it seems to be having a quiet snooze. Although the driver will engage it in conversation, when he chooses, it is not controlling the direction of the car.

Expository preaching puts the Bible firmly in the driving seat, at the wheel. It is the text which determines the content and direction of the sermon and the preacher becomes its willing servant. That is far from saying that he becomes merely a passive reactor. First, he has to receive and respond to the message of the text for himself. Understanding and assimilating its truth into his own life makes his relationship to the meaning and significance of the text highly active. Moreover, he will have many choices to make about how to present the text accurately and engagingly, how he will express its major ideas and how he will divide his time in the actual preaching. But in each of those choices it is the text that is in the driving-seat. That is what will dictate both the content and the shape of what is preached. Far from that producing some sort of inhibition or restriction on the preacher's individuality or creativity, it actually liberates him from the limitations and prejudices of his own restricted horizons, to revel in the infinite depth and variety of God's living and enduring Word.

## The Contemporary Crisis

This is not the place to argue for the inspiration and authority of the Scriptures, but it is, of course, the fundamental conviction of the expositor that the Bible in his hands is the unchanging and infallible Word of the living God. Expository preaching takes the Bible at face value, which is not the same as saying literalistically. It recognises different genres of Biblical writing, the place of metaphor and parable. It seeks always to interpret the text within its contexts—literary, historical and theological. It acknowledges the challenges of translation from the original languages. Its hermeneutic recognises that the starting point must always be to seek to understand, as clearly as possible, what this text meant to its author and his original hearers or readers, before we can ever begin to make valid appropriation of its unchanging truth to our contemporary situation. All of this is necessary preparation for the expositor and it will involve hard work, but that will never happen unless the conviction is embedded in the preacher's mind and heart that, 'All Scripture is breathed out by God and profitable for teaching, for reproof, for correction, and for training in righteousness, that the man of God may be competent, equipped for every good work' (2 Tim. 3:16-17). Only when that conviction dominates the preacher's mental and spiritual priorities will Paul's earlier exhortation to Timothy be taken seriously. 'Do your best to present yourself to God as one approved, a worker who has no need to be ashamed, rightly handling the word of truth' (2 Tim. 2:15).

You might be forgiven for thinking that this makes expository preaching what is often called a 'no brainer' choice for the evangelical preacher. But that is clearly not the case. Foremost among the contributory reasons for the lack of exposition is the contemporary crisis of preaching itself. Preaching currently has a very poor image. In part this is due to the deeper challenges of post-modernism regarding the credibility of Christianity in the contemporary world. Secular hostility towards preaching is partly philosophical in its origin and partly personal.

In a world where the only absolute is that there are no absolutes, what right does anyone have to assume the authority to tell me how to live my life? The concept of any overarching world view (such as Scripture), any metanarrative, that provides explanations and criteria by which to evaluate the truth or falsity of any set of beliefs has been widely rejected and derided. To claim the absolute nature of any kind of truth is regarded as arrogant since we cannot know everything about anything and so 'convictions' can at best be only provisional and must lack permanence. Not surprisingly, in this culture, preaching, whether from a pulpit ('six feet above contradiction') or from floor level, is seen as an archetypal example of the sort of control mechanisms and power ploys that lie at the heart of all religions. 'Don't preach at me!' has become a common expression of resistance to any intrusion into an individual's personal, private world.

Such a prevalent cultural 'given' is constantly penetrating and infecting the church, through its impact on individual members. In many contexts, preaching is regarded as an optional extra to the Sunday agenda rather than its central ingredient. While it may have some comforting or uplifting effect on the faithful, it could equally easily be jettisoned. There is a quiet disillusionment with the sort of preaching that may be generally orthodox and emollient, but which becomes predictable, repetitive and largely ineffective. Any expectation of life-changing encounters with God have long since gone and the view develops that preaching changes neither the church nor the world.

All these pressures inevitably deprive the preacher of confidence in what he is doing. Can it really be worthwhile spending much time on preaching preparation, when there are so many pressing alternative needs clamouring for his energies? He may receive very little positive feedback and often feels that he has had less than adequate equipping for the task. Other aspects of ministry yield much higher levels of approval from the congregation and so the church gradually drifts towards the world's estimate of preaching. The pastor is less and less convinced about its effectiveness; it just doesn't appear to be productive enough. And so, in John Milton's words, 'The hungry sheep look up, and are not fed'.

## Getting to the Roots

Why is this of such critical importance? The answer begins by recognising that the church is led by its preaching ministry. What happens week by week in the pulpit will always have a profound impact on the spiritual vitality, or otherwise, of those sitting in the pews. If there is no clear and consistent Biblical exposition, the congregation will become spiritually directionless and eventually moribund, because it is being starved of the nourishment which can only come from God's Word. If the Bible is not in the driving seat then either the preacher or the congregation will be. If the preacher's preoccupation at all costs is with winning the approval and favour of the hearers, then they are in the driving seat. They are unlikely to hear anything that would challenge their prejudices or unsettle their lifestyles. There has to be nothing to offend, so there are unlikely to be hard truths or Biblical negatives on the sermon's agenda. When that happens, either control is taken by those in the congregation who shout the loudest, or else a 'lowest common denominator' mentality develops, in which only the least offensive truths can be tolerated.

It may take some time for the effects on this approach to preaching to become apparent, but they will. The effects will be unfed sheep, not being nourished on the balanced spiritual diet of the whole counsel of God in the Scriptures. As a result, they will soon become anaemic, run down and listless. Their spiritual energy levels will decline. Good food gives you an appetite for more good food, but fast food diet substitutes do not produce strength, or health, energy or perseverance. The symptoms begin to appear. It gets harder and harder to get people to commit to any form of regular Christian service, or even to the priority of regular Sunday attendance. Some will start to drift, while others who remain gradually find their hearts hardening, as they are less and less ruled by desire for Christ and His kingdom. Slowly, pastoral black holes begin to open up, as individuals and families are sucked in by the world, the flesh and the devil. Unattended casualties increase, because their basic spiritual needs are unmet, vitality begins to ebb away and more people are slipping out the back door than those coming in the front.

But the root of the problem is not in preaching as a methodology. That has been foundational to the life of the church ever since the beginning. 'Everyone is looking for you', the disciples told Jesus as his public ministry took off in Galilee. 'And he said to them, 'Let us go on to the next towns, that I may preach there also, for that is why I came out' (Mark 1:37-38). In the synagogue at Nazareth, he defines His mission purpose in terms of Isaiah's prophecy. 'The Spirit of the Lord is upon me because he has anointed me to proclaim good news to the poor. He has sent me to proclaim liberty to the captives and recovering of sight to the blind, to set at liberty those who are oppressed, to proclaim the year of the Lord's favour.' And he concludes, 'Today this Scripture has been fulfilled in your hearing' (Luke 4:18-21). When God came to earth in the incarnation of the Son, He came as a proclaimer, a preacher. This is hardly surprising when we recall that the creation itself comes into being through God's powerful Word. Again and again, in Genesis 1, the formula is repeated, 'And God said, 'Let there be....' and there was....' He is the speaking God—the only one who can, for He alone is the only true and living God. As salvation history unfolds it is always governed and explained through God's speech. Indeed, the whole Bible can be understood as God preaching God, to us. This is why the letter to the Hebrews can summarise all that has gone before in these words, 'Long ago, at many times and in many ways, God spoke to our fathers by the prophets, but in these last days he has spoken to us by his Son...' (Heb. 1:1-2).

The glory of the Bible is that it is God's authoritative self-revelation. He does not hide Himself in obscurity; He makes himself known. He does this through His active governance and intervention in our time-space history and by His words of prediction and explanation about His actions. So the God of the Bible does things, speaks words of explanation and through events and explanations reveals Himself to human beings, who are created in His image. That is why we make ourselves known to one another in the same ways, by our actions and our words, which are the means by which we form relationships with one another. We are reflecting the ways in which God establishes His relationship with us.

Listen to the apostle Peter. 'For we did not follow cleverly devised myths when we made known to you the power and coming of our Lord Jesus Christ, but we were eye-witnesses of his majesty. For when he received honour and glory from God the Father, and the voice was borne to him by the Majestic Glory, 'This is my beloved Son, with whom I am well pleased,' we ourselves heard this very voice borne from heaven, for we were with him on the holy mountain' (2 Pet. 1:16-18). There was an event, which we call the transfiguration, which must have been one of the greatest experiences of Peter's life. It was not imagined. It was not engineered by men. It was a divine intervention, by and from the Majestic Glory. Peter was a part of it, as were James and John, 'We were eye-witnesses of his majesty.' God acted, as He removed something of the veil which hid the majestic glory of Jesus throughout His earthly ministry, to give the disciples a brief glimpse of the eternal reality of God's glory in Christ. 'His face shone like the sun, and his clothes became white as light' (Matt. 17:2). '...intensely white, as no one on earth could bleach them' (Mark 9:3). But what were they to make of this divine action? They needed a word of proclamation (exposition) from God to explain and confirm its purpose, 'This is my beloved Son'. The divine event is explained by the divine word of proclamation. Peter testifies, 'We ourselves heard this very voice borne from Heaven.' We saw and we heard. Eye-witnesses became also ear-witnesses.

Peter's point, in the context of his letter, is that although this was a totally unique occurrence, it represents the way God has always communicated Himself to the world and will always communicate Himself to the world, through His inspired Word. 'No prophecy of Scripture comes from someone's own interpretation. For no prophecy was ever produced by the will of man, but men spoke from God as they were carried along by the Holy Spirit' (2 Pet. 1:20-21). The Bible writers were the mouthpieces of the speaking, self-revealing God. The preachers of that authoritative, enduring, eternal Word therefore have everything that is needed in time and for eternity in the Scriptures themselves. Our task is to be faithful to the revelation already given, neither to add to, nor subtract from, its message, but to speak 'the truth, the whole truth and nothing but the truth'. It was Jesus Himself who said, 'Heaven and earth will pass away, but my words will not pass away' (Mark 13:31).

## Why Exposition is Essential

The nature of the Scriptures as divinely inspired and authenticated is claimed and taught throughout the Bible. To summarise this pervasive argument we can refer to the apostle Paul's unambiguous affirmation about the 'sacred writings' in 2 Timothy 3. Their first purpose, he states, is 'to make you wise for salvation through faith in Christ Jesus' (v. 15). Salvation is the greatest need of every human being and it is to be found through Christ alone. 'All Scripture is breathed out by God and profitable for teaching, for reproof, for correction, and for training in righteousness, that the man of God may be competent, equipped for every good work' (vv. 16-17).

Clearly the 'man of God' here is the one, like Timothy, who has been called by God to lead, pastor and feed His flock. Paul is saying that in the Scriptures (for us this means all 66 books) the messenger of God has the totally reliable and sufficient 'equipment' for the work of the ministry. And that is why, immediately afterwards, Paul gives Timothy Christ's solemn charge, 'Preach the Word' (2 Tim. 4:2). The reason for this is that it is the Word that does the work. In its broadest terms that 'work' is to bring men and women to salvation, through faith in Christ Jesus (see 2 Tim. 1:8-11) and then to encourage and enable believers, through the ministry of the Word, to grow to maturity in Christ. Among Paul's descriptions in this letter of what it means to 'live a godly life in Christ Jesus' (3:12) is the image of the vessels in a great house, 'some for honourable use, some for dishonourable'. Some are of gold and silver; some of wood and clay. He continues, 'If anyone cleanses himself from what is dishonourable, he will be a vessel for honourable use' and then, defining the goal of the pastor-teacher's ministry of the Word, he describes just what that means—'set apart as holy, useful to the master of the house, ready for every good work' (2 Tim. 2:20-21).

Obviously, Biblical Word ministry is something more than the words of the minister, however talented, engaging, popular or stimulating he may seem to be. Isaiah was told, 'All flesh is grass, and all its beauty is like the flower of the field' (Isa. 40:6). Whatever the abilities and accomplishments of the preacher, they are only transitory and insubstantial. 'The grass withers, the flower fades, but the word of our God will stand forever' (Isa. 40:8). That is why the task is not simply to preach, but to preach the Word. All the content needed to bring men and women to faith and to grow them in likeness to Christ, as the image of God is being restored, is already there in the Scriptures, as they are expounded. There is a dynamic life-giving power in the Word of God in the hands of the Spirit of God, who inspired its writers and who illuminates and enables its hearers. As Jesus himself taught us, 'It is the Spirit who gives life, the flesh is of no avail. The words that I have spoken to you are spirit and life' (John 6:63). So the preacher's task is to sit under the authority of the Word, humbly seeking to understand the text in its context, and then to stand behind the Word as he opens the pages of Scripture and offers its meaning and messages to the congregation.

Expository preaching is the God-ordained and Spirit-enabled means by which the church grows and flourishes, both in the addition of new believers and towards maturity in Christ. It is not merely an option, but the essential. One of the most stimulating of the many books I have read on preaching is John Piper's 1990 Baker Book House volume entitled, *The Supremacy of God in Preaching*. In it, the author reminds us of a sentence of Cotton Mather, the New England Puritan of 300 years ago, which has stayed with me ever since I first read it. In his book *Student and Preacher* (1726) Mather wrote, 'The great design and intention of the office of a Christian preacher [is] to restore the throne and dominion of God in the souls of men.' That is a sentence worth pondering, to humble us, challenge and invigorate us, as we feel something of Paul's sense of inadequacy when he asked 'Who is sufficient for these things?' Mather's sentence came from his consideration of Romans 10:14-15, a famous exploration of the necessity of preaching, culminating in the quotation of Isaiah 52:7 as it is written, 'How beautiful are the feet of those who preach the good news'. Setting that verse in its Old Testament context, Mather realised that the gospel of salvation, peace and happiness is summed up in the message of the last three words of the verse, 'Your God reigns'. That is what shaped Mather's 'great design.'

In an extended application, Piper comments, 'The keynote in the mouth of every prophet-preacher, whether in Isaiah's day or Jesus' day or our day, is "Your God Reigns!"' (p. 22). He continues,

> The implication for preaching is plain: When God sends his emissaries to declare, "Your God reigns!" his aim is not to constrain man's submission by an act of raw authority; his aim is to ravish our affections with irresistible displays of glory. The only submission that fully reflects the worth and glory of the King is glad submission... The only submission to the lordship of Christ that fully magnifies his worth and reflects his beauty is the humble gladness of the human soul in the glory of God in the face of his Son (pp. 25-26).

That is why expository preaching matters so much, since its expression of God's self-revelation in all the Scriptures is the means God has chosen to make known His kingly glory, His sovereign rule, throughout the world. Can you think of anything more exciting or fulfilling than to be allowed just a tiny fraction of a part in God's eternal plans, the biggest picture of all? What greater motivation could there possibly be?

# 2
# Practising the Method

Expository preaching takes the Bible so seriously that it ensures the Bible is in the driving-seat of the sermon. But are we saying that expository preaching is the only way? And what does it mean in practice to be committed to this as the heart of our ministry? As we examine the answer to the second question I think the answer to the first will become clear.

## Initial Comments

We start with the premise that God is the perfect communicator (how could it be otherwise?) and that the Bible is His perfect self-revelation in both its contents and its method. It is the supreme means by which we can come to a true knowledge of God and in that personal, relational knowledge of God, 'his divine power has granted to us all things that pertain to life and godliness' (2 Pet. 1:3). Since God Himself has chosen to communicate Himself in this way, our task as His ministers (servants) is to work hard at understanding its contents and message and to pray that as we seek to preach and expound Scripture, God's voice will be authentically heard. This requires discipline and sacrifice. It is not my voice, not the bees buzzing in my bonnet, not even my explanation of the text that shape the content or direction of the preaching. I don't have to do something with the Bible text. I don't have to try to make it relevant through pop psychology or by generating emotional warmth. I have to let the Bible text first do something with me and in me as I receive and respond to its message in my own life. And I don't have to make it relevant because it already is. It is the 'living and abiding word of God' (1 Pet. 1:23), so how could it not be the most relevant document anyone could read, the most important message anyone could hear?

But having a bag of tools is very different from being a skilled craftsman. A surgical procedure may be very well documented and proven, but the surgeon does not pick up the ability to perform it with precision by the odd half-hour or two on the internet. That requires hard work and grows increasingly with experience. So Paul's charge to Timothy is highly relevant for all gospel ministers. 'Do your best to present yourself to God as one approved, a worker who has no need to be ashamed, rightly handling the word of truth' (2 Tim. 2:15). There are several important observations to make about this key verse. First, the Christian pastor is to be a worker. It is a demanding life-work. Next, his work is carried out in the knowledge that it will be assessed by God. He does not want to fail that test. He wants to be approved, having met God's standards and proving to be a genuine and faithful steward. And that is why he does his best. He concentrates his attention and energy on doing the job as well as he possibly can. The fact that he knows that it is only God who gives the increase is no excuse for his laziness or half-heartedness, because he is responsible for his own use of God's resources and the task is very demanding. Lastly, both the task and the criterion for assessment is described as 'rightly handling the word of truth'. The literal meaning of the verb is to cut straight and the word of truth signifies 'the pattern of the sound words', 'the good deposit entrusted to you' by the apostle (see 2 Tim. 1:13-14). John Stott comments, 'For us it is quite simply, Scripture. To 'cut it straight' or 'make it a straight path' is to be accurate on the one hand and plain on the other in our exposition.... [The good workman] handles the word with such scrupulous care that he both stays on the path himself, keeping to the highway and avoiding the byways, and makes it easy for others to follow'.[1]

I remember hearing John Stott, when I was a theological student, answer a question about the secret of his expository ministry, by saying that there were three. The first was hard work, the second more hard work and the third....! Yet it is the most fulfilling hard work that any of us could be involved in. It yields eternal dividends. But it is this hard work that is perhaps the greatest deterrent to quality expository preaching, in our age of sound bites and quick fixes. One of the secrets of an effective expository ministry I have discovered is diary control. You cannot do this work unless you set aside sufficient time for it and that time will not just appear miraculously from nowhere. It has to be diarised. It's all a matter of priorities. If the hungry sheep are to be fed, you will need to set aside a number of non-negotiable study times in the week before you preach.

---

1    *The Message of 2 Timothy* IVP, 1973, pp. 67-68.

When I was a local church pastor, I aimed for two-and-a half hours in the study, for four mornings in the week. Everyone will develop their own pattern, but expository preaching takes time in the preparation and there are plenty of other competing demands that will erode that time, if you do not guard it. But I know that I served my congregation best when I prepared best.

## Working on the Text

As we follow some of the preparation patterns which we need to develop if we are to become expository preachers, I hope that we shall also see how greatly this approach will benefit our congregations.

Firstly, expository preaching deals with the Bible in the way that God has put it together and presents it to us, which is book by book. All the recent surveys show a sharp decline in the practice of private Bible reading or study among Christians, so that we are faced in the churches with a growing problem of Biblical illiteracy. In the case of many who are coming to faith from a totally secular background there is often no understanding of the Bible at all. I think it is highly likely that pulpit practices may have a negative effect on this. The Bible is a complex (but not complicated) library of sixty-six individual books, each with its own distinctive message contributing to the whole overarching story from Genesis to Revelation. We can easily forget how daunting it can appear. Many Christians know only a handful of verses, usually the choices of Christian calendars, or a selection of favourite stories. If the preaching they hear takes Bible passages disconnected from their book context, or gathered together from various parts of the Bible to illustrate a particular chosen theme, their understanding of the Bible is always going to be at best piecemeal and inadequate.

Preachers will frequently say that their congregation cannot 'take' a series through a book; they will become bored and disengaged. But isn't this dangerously near to saying that we know better than God does about how to nurture His people? He could have written us a book of systematic theology, but He didn't. He might have provided us with a series of uplifting anecdotes, but He didn't. Instead, He provided us with sixty-six books, set at different periods in salvation history, written by a variety of authors to a wide range of audiences, employing different literary genres, but each with its own distinctive message and purpose. God selected and preserved each one because of its unique contribution to our understanding of His character and knowledge of His purposes. So, if I choose to take just one chapter out of its book for a short sermon series, followed by a month of psalms, followed by some key episodes from the life of Abraham, followed by a short series on prayer or the second coming, I can claim that I am being Biblical in my preaching, but I am not being thoroughly committed to exposition. Whereas, if I am working my way systematically through a book, I am able to set the text in its book context and see how that relates both to the bigger Biblical metanarrative and to the parallels in our own situation. Consecutive exposition teaches the text in its context and concentrates on the distinctive ingredients of this particular book, along with the author's pastoral intention. It builds the understanding week by week and the hearers begin to learn the Bible book by book.

Of course, this does not mean that one should necessarily work one's way through a long book of the Bible from beginning to end. Much depends on the condition of the congregation. There is no reason why a longer book cannot be subdivided into sections, which would enable it to be visited consecutively in several series over a few years. A major book like Isaiah, for example, could be divided into five parts (1-12, 13-27, 28-39, 40-55 and 56-66), each series perhaps occupying a three-month period over successive years.

## The Importance of Context

Next, expository preaching forces the preacher to pay attention to the contexts so that the book's intended, authentic message is clearly heard. We all know that 'a text out of context becomes a pretext for a proof text', but when that happens it greatly reduces the authority of the sermon and, by association, that of the Bible too. This is very dangerous, because it undermines the hearers' confidence and faith in the Word. The response is often, 'Well, I didn't see where he got that idea from', or 'That's just the preacher's interpretation; I have my own'.

Recognising that every passage of Scripture is set within its own context both in its book and in the whole Bible, the expositor is acutely aware that meaning is not exclusively determined by vocabulary and sentence structures, but also by position and purpose. So his study will look at what immediately precedes and follows the passage being studied, in order to determine why what is being said belongs to *this* place in the book's argument or storyline. Context questions will include, 'Why does the author use these particular words to convey his meaning?' Again, 'Why does he say it to these people (his original hearers) at this point in the development of the book and in their own history?' As we begin to understand what it meant to them then, we shall begin to see how it can relate to us now. Context provides application for the expositor, as we see the parallels between the original audience and our own situation, although we are at a very different point along the historical timeline. This means that he does not have to find some external application from his contemporary evangelical sub-cultural framework to bolt on to the text. Rather, in exploring the original context and then relating that into the whole Bible context, the relevance and intended application of this particular passage becomes increasingly clear.

## An Example of Context

It may be helpful at this point to use an illustrative example, to demonstrate how the expository method can develop and deepen the understanding of a whole book and enrich our experience of its message. In this case a single phrase, when carefully explored, opens up a much wider vista.

Studying to preach Ephesians 1 quickly brings one to a key phrase in verse 3. The context is the beginning of the great ascription of praise to God, 'who has blessed us in

Christ with every spiritual blessing in the heavenly places'. It would be very easy to take the phrase 'in the heavenly places' to refer to the future reality we commonly call 'heaven' and to recognise that all the blessings of eternity are to be found 'in Christ'. But the unusual nature of the phrase prompts us to look further. A lexicon helps us to see that the phrase is literally 'the heavenlies' and when we consult a concordance we discover that, unusually, the phrase occurs several times in this letter and rarely elsewhere in Paul. But what does it mean? Clearly, the blessings that are listed in the verses that follow begin to be experienced here, in this life, even if their ultimate fulfilment will be in the world to come.

Remembering that Bible words have Bible meanings, the expositor begins to explore the meaning of the phrase by studying its use elsewhere in the letter. Later in chapter 1, reflecting on the 'immeasurable greatness' of God's power demonstrated in Christ's resurrection, Paul describes Him as 'seated at his (the Father's) right hand in the heavenly places, far above all rule and authority and power and dominion' (1:20-21). This location where Jesus reigns might feasibly mean 'heaven', but chapter 2 uses the same language to describe the Christian's present experience. 'God made us alive together with Christ ... and raised us up with him and seated us with him in the heavenly places in Christ Jesus.' (2:5-6). That would seem to speak of a present reality. And the same must be true in 3:10, where Paul affirms that 'through the church the manifold wisdom of God might now be made known to the rulers and authorities in the heavenly places'.

Are these angelic beings, or human potentates? The final chapter provides the answer. 'For we do not wrestle against flesh and blood, but against the rulers, against the authorities, against the cosmic powers over this present darkness, against the spiritual forces of evil in the heavenly places. Therefore take up the whole armour of God ....' (6:12-13). The evil powers have no place or part in the heaven of heavens, God's dwelling-place, but they do operate and exercise a limited power in what Paul calls 'the heavenlies'. This is the area in which the spiritual battle rages, prosecuted by the devil and his forces against Christ and His kingdom. The whole letter affirms that there is not the slightest doubt about the ultimate outcome, since the risen Christ has 'ascended far above all the heavens, that he might fill all things' (4:10).

So why this emphasis in this letter? Comparing Scripture with Scripture, one of the expositor's essential tools, we are taken back to the first planting of the church in Ephesus, in Acts chapter 19. This was the city where 'God was doing extraordinary miracles by the hands of Paul' (v. 11) as the tangible manifestation of the power of Christ. In His name, diseases were cured and evil spirits exorcised. 'And fear fell upon them all, and the name of the Lord Jesus was extolled' (v. 17). This was the city where the great bonfire of their magic books, spells and incantations, kindled by the new believers, amounted in value to fifty thousand pieces of silver (v. 18-19). This was where Paul 'persuaded and turned away a great many people saying that gods made with hands are not gods' (v. 26) and where her devotees feared 'that the temple of the great goddess Artemis may be counted as nothing and that she may even be deposed from her magnificence, she whom all Asia and the world worship' (v. 27). Ephesus was a spiritual battle-ground, the location of a cosmic conflict.

The emphasis throughout the letter on the total supremacy of Christ over all the hostile spiritual powers is needed to give the new believers the assurance that they share in Christ's victory and that no demonic agency can overcome those whose trust is in Christ and who are wearing 'the whole armour of God'. Exploration of the text, in its book context, reveals that Christ's people are secure in time and for eternity because they are 'in him', as they anticipate the fulfilment of God's purposes, His 'plan for the fulness of time, to unite all things in him, things in heaven and things on earth' (1:10). Meanwhile, the church, in its unity as the one body of the one Lord, is the outcrop in time of what will be the fulness of God's plan in eternity—Jew and Gentile are one in Christ Jesus.

Expository work of this sort immediately begins to open up powerful applications to our own context today. We may not live in the occult sink that was Ephesus, but we certainly know the powerful hostility of the god of this world as he blinds the minds of unbelievers to keep them from seeing the light of the gospel and as he propagates his destructive lies throughout our culture and society. The assurances of the letter, as they are expounded, provide contemporary believers with the confidence we need to keep trusting and obeying our victorious Lord in all the conflicts that we face.

Context study helps us to move from meaning to significance, as we appreciate the authorial intention behind the passage, inspired of course by the Holy Spirit. But we don't preach the context. The study of context is designed to illuminate the text, but the text is the subject of the preaching. There is an important point here with regard to preaching Old Testament texts to New Testament believers. We have to remember that since the coming of Christ and the revelation of the gospel, we have to read the Old through the lens of the New, the lens of Christ's person and work. The whole Bible context is therefore important, since it underlines that we are not in the same position as the old covenant community of Israel. For example, God's covenant of grace is no longer focussed on ethnic Israel, but comprises an innumerable multitude from every tribe and nation. But it can be a trap for preachers who are well schooled in Biblical theology to use Old Testament passages, rather like a trampoline, to bounce off as quickly as possible to Christ and the gospel. Such preaching can become all too predictable and ultimately boring, which is a travesty of its true purpose. The expositor will use the Biblical theological context rightly to apply the Old Testament truth, but he will not preach the context. Rather, he will use the unique detail of each passage to highlight different aspects of Christ's glory in the gospel. Preachers are sometimes taught that they should ask the question of every Old Testament text, 'Where is Jesus in this text?' The intention is good, but it can tend to promote very inventive and individualistic answers. I would suggest that a better way is to frame the question, 'What difference does it make to this Old Testament text that Jesus has come?'

## Beware of Imposition

Next, expository preaching helps to counteract our natural tendency as preachers to impose our own framework on the text. The story of the preacher who told his colleague, 'I've got a wonderful sermon. All I need now is to find a text to hang it on,' is often not so far from the truth. It comes from the preacher being in the driving-seat. He decides that he knows what his congregation 'needs', which may or may not be true. It is important to exegete the target audience as well as the Biblical passage, so that we are enabled to communicate its message as persuasively and effectively as we can to our hearers. But that is not what decides the content of the sermon. In expository preaching the text is king.

However, we cannot approach any Biblical text without our multi-faceted framework coming into play. When you wear a pair of sunglasses you see everything through the tinted lenses. There is no other way of looking at anything. The lenses condition your entire perception of reality. Similarly, we never approach a Biblical text without reading it through our own habitual lenses, which will be determined by many different factors of life experience, cultural norms, theological convictions, and so on. These all contribute to the framework or mind-set that we bring to the Bible, which will be unique to each individual preacher, although it will have many common ingredients with the framework of others. The danger is that it will impose itself upon the text, so that the resulting sermon may look to the text to support the preacher's own ideas, but will not primarily expound its meaning and significance.

Framework preaching is agenda preaching and that is certainly easier than exposition and can sometimes suggest to us that it will also be more 'relevant'. Dedicated church leaders inevitably have agendas which they long to see fulfilled in their congregation. Under the pressure of so many demands on their time textual preparation is skimped, the framework takes over and the prevailing concerns they have begin to dominate the preaching. The framework may be about certain favourite doctrines, or it may keep coming back to the 'simple gospel'. Often, it is concerned with the life of the congregation in terms of seeking to impose certain patterns of behaviour. This sort of preaching frequently operates with a challenging formula: 'Are you doing... enough?' Are you having your quiet times, giving, evangelising, attending a small group? The list could be lengthened. And, of course, all these are very good things to highlight, but have you noticed how largely ineffective such preaching becomes?

The reason why this sort of framework preaching fails to change people is because its authority depends upon the preacher and its content becomes repetitious and predictable. From which, the next stage is congregational boredom and switch-off. As Spurgeon is said to have commented about certain preachers in his own day, 'Ten-thousand-thousand are their texts, but all their sermons one!' The sheep are not being fed. Indeed, rather, if the preacher persists in this, with increasing fervour because of its ineffectiveness, they are being thrashed. That is not what Christ commanded and the prophet Ezekiel had some searching things to say from God about shepherds who used the flock for their own ends (Ezek. 34:1-6). The weaker hearers buckle under the pressure, while the rest begin to develop a resistance to what is preached, neither of which is a desirable outcome. Agenda preaching imposes applications from outside the passage on the hearers, but these have no lasting validity unless they can be shown to emerge consequentially from the meaning of the text. It is the applicatory significance of the Scriptures, not the framework of the preacher, which will prevent us from viewing the Word of God through the defective lens of our own contemporary situation.

Expository preaching disciplines us constantly to ask questions of the text, not to impose our ideas on it. By this process in preparation, the preacher's own framework is always being challenged, refreshed or changed. So whenever he comes across something in the text which questions his framework, there is the possibility of growth and development. He learns to stop on those searching questions. 'Why does he say that here? Why in these words? I wouldn't have said that or expressed it that way. It seems odd to me. What's happening here?' These are the questions that will produce fresh and faithful preaching and which will make the preacher's own framework increasingly true to Scripture. Over time this produces a preacher whose blood is 'Bibline'.[2]

---

2.   'Mr. Spurgeon as a Literary Man,' in *The Autobiography of Charles H. Spurgeon, Compiled from His Letters, Diaries, and*

It was said of John Bunyan that if you cut him the Bible would flow out of his veins. That's something to aim for!

## Increasing in the Knowledge of God

A further value of expository preaching is that the congregation is being nurtured with the balanced diet, prescribed by the Lord Himself, in His provision of the whole Bible. Systematic consecutive exposition of the Scripture ensures that over a period of time those ingredients which are most common are treated with greater regularity, while the more peripheral ingredients occur much more rarely. You may have to wait some time to hear a sermon on the head coverings in 1 Corinthians 11, but because the whole Bible is God's preaching God to us, teaching about His divine character and work should occur somewhere in every sermon. So among the first questions the expositor will be asking of any text is 'What is God teaching us about God here?' This may concern the Father, the Son, the Holy Spirit, or the whole Trinity, but it will always be true to the ultimate self-revelatory purposes of God in speaking these words. He wants us to know this about himself.

All good preaching begins with good listening. And listening attentively is achieved by asking questions. Start with God. The Bible is God's book about Himself before it is His book about us. Our cultural conditioning makes us assume that it is all about us and so imposes our world on to the understanding of the text. The result is that much of

*Records by His Wife and Private Secretary*, vol. 4, 1878-1892 (Curtis & Jennings, 1900), p. 268.

the preaching diet focusses on us, our needs, our feelings, our circumstances. If we are too much in the foreground of the sermon, you can be sure that God will be in the background, albeit wheeled in ultimately, like some 'deus ex machina', as the solution to the problems that preoccupy us. For example, the Old Testament prophets are very concerned about the oppression and suffering being caused to Israel by the Assyrian dominance and then to Judah by the Babylonian ascendancy. But the thrust of their message is to expose the idolatrous worship among God's people, which is causing His judgement to fall on them, by the removal of His protection from their enemies. However, if the preacher is not listening to the text in its context, as God teaches the hearers about Himself, he will be tempted to major on the human suffering, because that is what preoccupies the modern hearer. But God is dethroned.

Because God is not presented as the sovereign mover, as the context teaches and demands, in all the majesty of His rule and authority, governing the nations and accomplishing His universal and eternal purposes, He becomes simply the comforter of His people in the midst of our problems, which then fill the picture. Under this sort of preaching God becomes pocket-sized, existing merely to meet our needs. And because in a fallen world like this those needs will always be with us, and sometimes multiplying, we begin to think that He doesn't know or He doesn't care. The God who is diminished by such unbalanced preaching will gradually begin to fade out of our perception, like the Cheshire cat in *Alice in*

*Wonderland.* Expository preaching allows God to set the agenda, so that truths about God and His significance, rather than the terms of the human condition, will predominate. As J. I. Packer has said, the proper aim of preaching is to mediate meetings with God.

## Growing Better Grass

One final addition to the values of expository preaching is that it shows the congregation how to study the Bible for themselves. This is something that is perhaps caught rather than taught. For myself, my appetite for Scripture was enormously increased in my student days by hearing faithful exposition. And once you have been fed on quality food, you will never go back to the quick-fire takeaway. John Stott used to make the point so well when he said that sheep need rich, nourishing pasture, while goats will eat anything. Expository ministry grows greener grass and will always draw hungry sheep to feed on God's riches. Make no mistake about it, there are very many hungry Christians today who are longing to be fed from God's Word, but sadly finding only very limited pasture.

However, while the preacher is to provide good grazing for the flock, he also wants them to learn how to feed themselves and there can be little doubt that clear expository ministry will produce Bible-loving, Bible-studying and Bible-obedient local churches. This is because consistent exposition opens up consecutive passages and whole books to the hearers, by showing them the content of the meaning and its implications for life. Application is really helping the hearers to work on, and then work out, the life implications of what is being taught in the text. In the course of an expository preaching ministry all the different genres of the Biblical literature will be covered. The congregation will learn to read Biblical narratives in order to discover the turning point of each story so that the reason for its being told, the teaching point, will become clear. Biblical prophecy will not be regarded merely as 'history written in advance,' but rather as God teaching about the future consequences of present actions (or refusal to act) in the context of His own eternal plan. Understanding its significance to the first hearers will prompt us to see its future fulfilment in the coming of the Lord Jesus Christ and, through His person and work, in the eternal kingdom yet to be consummated.

These are simply examples of how exposition helps to equip Bible hearers to be Bible readers and students, who themselves 'rightly handle the word of truth'. That should surely be the preacher's aim if like Paul he is convinced that his ministry call is to 'present everyone mature in Christ' (Col. 1:28). Other genres such as law, wisdom, gospels, epistles and apocalyptic will all be treated in the course of regular exposition, so that for the hearers the Bible moves from being merely a pick 'n' mix tub of favourite verses, spiritual sweeties to suck, with some other difficult parts we never look at, to the whole counsel of God, the inexhaustible riches of His self-revelation, the greatest treasure that this world can afford.

## Going for Gold

So is expository preaching the only way? No, but I would want to stake a claim that it is the best way. It is the gold standard. It will provide the best staple diet for any local church congregation and you will never run out of material! But, more importantly, the work of preparing and preaching exposition will keep the preacher believing and obeying God's Word himself, as he is challenged, rebuked, corrected, refreshed and equipped by its penetrating truth. As Paul told Timothy, 'Keep a close watch on yourself and on the teaching.' (The two go together.) 'Persist in this, for by so doing you will save both yourself and your hearers' (1 Tim. 4:16). It guarantees honesty, authenticity and above all progress, as an unashamed worker. Godly pastors are created and preserved by the work of exposition.

Fifty years ago, the German pastor and preacher, Helmut Thielicke, published a book entitled *The Trouble with the Church*. He was prompted to ask why the Reformation view of preaching as 'the source and spring of Christian faith' had largely disappeared from post-war Europe. Among a variety of reasons, Thielicke identified a central issue relating to the ministers, the preachers themselves. He asked, 'Does the preacher really live in the house of the dogmas he proclaims? Does all the rest of his life (out of the pulpit and the church) relate to that house?' He was asking questions about personal priorities, the centre of gravity, because he knew that 'where your treasure is there will your heart be also'. He was enquiring whether the preacher lived any longer in 'the house of his utterance'. Expository preaching will keep us to that sort of authenticity.

It seems counter-intuitive to many that the exposition of texts nearly two thousand years old, and more, could possibly connect with the modern world. And yet when it is practised we see over and over again that is precisely what happens. The Bible has always been under attack; by rationalism in the eighteenth century, liberalism in the nineteenth, scepticism and materialism in the twentieth and now post-modern relativism and rampant secularism in the twenty-first, to name but a few of its foes. Yet multitudes of lives around the world affirm that in the proclamation of the Word of God they have truly heard the voice of God. What John Calvin affirmed in his sermon on 1 Timothy 3:2 ('Apt to teach') remains true. 'For St. Paul does not mean that one should just make a parade here or that a man should show off so that everyone applauds him and says, "Oh! Well-spoken! Oh! What a breadth of learning! Oh! What a subtle mind." All that is beside the point....When a man has climbed up into the pulpit, is it so that he may be seen from afar, and that he may be pre-eminent? Not at all. It is that God may speak to us by the mouth of a man.' As he goes on to develop the idea elsewhere, 'We shall not hear only a mortal man speaking but we shall feel, even by God's secret power, that God is speaking to our souls, that he is the teacher. He so touches us that the human voice enters into us and so profits us that we are refreshed and nourished by it.'[3]

---

3    Quoted in T. H. L. Parker's *Calvin's Preaching* 1992, p. 42.

The expository preacher believes that the Spirit of God takes the Word of God to accomplish the work of God. He believes that if he is faithfully proclaiming the Scripture, which is the Word of God, God's voice will be truly heard. The ability of the preacher, either intellectually or oratorically, will neither determine, nor limit, its efficacy. Because it is God who speaks through His Word on the lips of the preacher, it means that Scripture must always be the non-negotiable constant in preaching and exposition the only valid method.

# 3
## Embracing the Whole Bible

If the expository method is so central to the wellbeing of the church we should expect to find that corroborated within the Bible itself by what we see of the practice of preaching. We shall not be disappointed. We need to look at some examples to give us this confidence.

## The Early Foundations

In the Old Testament, the major preachers are the prophets. Although their messages come to us in written form, it is obvious that they were originally delivered orally. Their oracles are like summary sermons and it is instructive to see how they operated. Moses, the first great prophet, who spoke with God, face to face, as a man speaks with his friend, receives the law from God to pass it on to the people and it is on that basis that the covenant is established (Exod. 24:3-8). That law is enshrined in the Book of the Covenant, to which after its public reading the people respond, 'All that the Lord has spoken we will do, and we will be obedient'. After the death of Moses, as the nation enters the promised land, under Joshua, their future is to be governed by this written Word of law, the Torah (instruction). 'This Book of the Law shall not depart from your mouth, but you shall meditate on it day and night, so that you may be careful to do according to all that is written in it. For then you will make your way prosperous, and then you will have good success.' (Josh. 1:8)

When the writing prophets are sent from God, during the centuries of Israel's decline encompassing the destruction of the northern kingdom by the Assyrians and culminating in the Babylonian exile of the southern kingdom, they do not come as the bearers of fresh revelation, but as preachers of the revelation already given. Their message is directly given by God, of course, and its content totally controlled by Him. But their role is to speak as God's agents, as what Gordon Fee and Douglas Stuart call 'covenant enforcement mediators'.[1] They are mediators because they come from the presence of God with His Word as an act of grace towards His rebellious people. However, they come on the basis of the covenant, the already written revelation, to enforce obedience, by presenting the alternatives of covenant blessings or curses, of fulfilment or judgement, in terms of the current situation in which their hearers are placed. In castigating the false prophets whom God did not send, but who took to themselves the responsibility of speaking vain hopes to the people, Jeremiah speaks for the Lord, who defines the nature and purpose of true prophecy, as over against the false, in these terms. 'I did not send the prophets, yet they ran; I did not speak to them, yet they prophesied. But if they had stood in my council, then they would have proclaimed my words to my people, and they would have turned them from their evil way, and from

---

1     *How to Read the Bible for All its Worth*, Zondervan 2014.

the evil of their deeds' (Jer. 23:21-22). The prophets are expounding and applying the already existing revelation with powerful penetration to their own times.

As the grand overarching themes of the Old Testament are unfolded down the centuries, the Bible introduces us to its own principle of progressive, or perhaps better, cumulative revelation. The appearance of a new book never alters the existing revelation. It may point to a clearer fulfilment, but we never have to unlearn anything from the earlier revelation since the nature of the God who has spoken is unchanging. The earlier revelation must always be interpreted in the light of the later revelation, as the focus sharpens with the passage of time, but the unchanging content of that earlier revelation is the foundation on which the latter is built.

It is the nature of Old Testament Scripture that the prophets are proclaiming the fresh revelation given to them directly from the Lord. No contemporary preacher has (or needs) that privilege, because what was revealed to them has been recorded for us, 'that through endurance and through the encouragement of the Scriptures we might have hope' (Rom. 15:4). But implicit in that is the conviction that every word matters and that the explanation of the mind of God revealed in the past depends upon the detail of the text in its exposition. For example, Amos 4:6-11 is a series of powerful indictments of Israel's unfaithfulness, which must inevitably call out God's judgement ('Prepare to meet your God', 4:12). The details list famine, drought, blight, plague, military defeat and overthrown cities. In each case the same refrain occurs, 'Yet you have not returned to me, declares the Lord'. What should they have learned from these calamities? They were covenant judgements exactly as listed in the earlier revelation of Leviticus 26:14ff as divine punishment for disobedience. It was a key passage which young Jewish boys would have learned by heart. Amos is preaching its specific content to them in detail, not just as a general concept, because the text was already in their memory bank.

Perhaps the most specific Old Testament example we have of what we would now call expository method comes after the return from the Babylonian exile, when the walls of Jerusalem had finally been rebuilt, as recorded in Nehemiah 8. An assembly is called of 'both men and women and all who could understand what they heard', to listen to Ezra, the scribe, reading from the Book of the Law. Standing on a wooden platform above the people, Ezra read God's holy Word 'from early morning until midday', but simply reading the text was not sufficient. Dividing the people into smaller units, it was the task of the Levites to help the people to understand (v. 7). 'They read from the book, from the Law of God, clearly, and they gave the sense so that the people understood the reading.' (v. 8). All the words mattered and all the people needed to hear and understand their exposition. It seems to have been the standard method.

## Jesus and the Scriptures

The supreme example for us must of course be how the Lord Jesus handled the Scriptures when He came into the world to inaugurate the new covenant through His death and resurrection. Gathering His disciples, as the foundation of the new Israel, Jesus tells them, 'Do not think that I have come to abolish the Law or the Prophets; I have not come to abolish them but to fulfil them.' (Matt. 5:17). His was not a ministry of replacement, but fulfilment, as is indicated by the many times He explained His actions in terms of the details of an Old Testament text. In fact, He is recorded as quoting Old Testament Scriptures at least 78 times in the gospels, from 15 different books.

Although Jesus came supremely to be a preacher (Mark 1:38), He is of course of a totally different quality from any of His apostles, or us, as their successors. This is because He is in Himself the living Word, made flesh, revealing God's glory, 'full of grace and truth' (John 1:14). Because all the Old Testament Scriptures point to Him as the focus and centre of the revelation and because all the promises of God find their fulfilment in Him, He is in Himself the fullest exposition of those Scriptures. As Paul later said, 'All the promises of God find their Yes in him (Christ). That is why it is through him that we utter our Amen to God for his glory' (2 Cor. 1:20). It would hardly be surprising if Jesus had chosen simply to reveal His power and glory without reference to Scripture – except that that is never God's way. He always directs His people to put their faith in His written Word, to lead them to the living Word.

Think how Jesus uses Scripture, for example, in Matthew 12:40-42. Taking the narrative of Jonah as historic fact, He uses its details ('three days and nights in the belly of the great fish') to foretell His death and resurrection, the point being that the detail of the text is expounded in Jesus Himself. 'Behold something greater than Jonah is here'. The same point is made about His fulfilment of the wisdom of Solomon which the Queen of Sheba came to hear. 'Behold something greater than Solomon is here.' He does not expand the detail exegetically, but He expounds its meaning and significance in terms of his own unique presence and divinity. And the same sort of exposition governs His post-resurrection instruction of the disciples. To the two on their way to Emmaus, 'beginning with Moses and all the Prophets, he interpreted to them in all the Scriptures the things concerning himself' (Luke 24:27). Later, to the gathered disciples, he declared 'that everything written about me in the Law of Moses and the Prophets and the Psalms must be fulfilled.' And Luke explains, 'Then he opened their minds to understand the Scriptures' (Luke 24:44-45). Even though they do not have the written text in front of them at this time, clearly his teaching method is expository.

But on one occasion, right at the start of His ministry, we do find Him with the scroll in His hand, reading from what we call Isaiah 61:1-2, in the synagogue at Nazareth. 'The Spirit of the Lord is upon me, because he has anointed me', which has a threefold proclamation effect, of good news to the poor, liberty to the captives and the year of the Lord's favour. As He sits to preach, Jesus claims, 'Today this Scripture has been fulfilled in your hearing' (Luke 4:17-21). Clearly, His proclamation is governed by the detail of the text which He is expounding, because Luke tells us that He ended its reading before the completion of the original sentence. In Isaiah it continues 'and the day of vengeance of our God'. But that day was still future, not fulfilled that day in Nazareth, and so Jesus ends the text before its announcement. His preaching was entirely governed and defined by the wording of the text, because His foundational methodology was expository.

For the apostles to be able to emulate their master, they would need the gift of the promised Spirit of truth to be with them forever, as their teacher and interpreter. So Jesus told them, 'He will teach you all things and bring to your remembrance all that I have said to you' (John 14:26). And again, 'When the Spirit of truth comes, he will guide you into all the truth .... He will glorify me, for he will take what is mine and declare it to you' (John 16:13-14). The teaching of Jesus was the fulfilment of all that the prophets foretold. Peter writes that they were on tiptoes seeking to find out more about the gospel and the coming of the Christ. 'It was revealed to them that they were serving not themselves but you, in the things that have now been announced to you through those who preached the good news to you by the Holy Spirit sent from heaven, things into which angels long to look.' (1 Pet. 1:12)

Moving in to the New Testament era we have the centrality of Biblical explanation brought before us in two ways. Firstly we have the record of the earliest Christian ministry, detailed for us in Luke's account in Acts. Secondly, we have the evidence of the epistles themselves, as 'the pattern of sound words', which form the inspired apostolic instruction for the church. And in both cases the method is expository.

## The Apostolic Pattern

Paul's second missionary journey provides us with invaluable evidence about both the content and methodology of the apostolic preaching. In chapters 17-20 we follow Paul's progress to Thessalonica, Berea, Athens, Corinth and eventually to Ephesus. Wherever possible he begins with a synagogue, 'as was his custom', but we also see him at the Areopagus in Athens and the lecture hall of Tyrannus in Ephesus. What is so instructive is the use of the verbs Luke employs to describe his ministry. In the synagogue at Thessalonica 'he reasoned with them from the Scriptures' (Acts 17:11) and the content here was clearly expository, 'explaining and proving' the necessity of the cross and proclaiming that Jesus is the Christ (v. 3). The response verb is also striking. Luke tells us that 'some of them were persuaded and joined Paul and Silas, as did a great many of the devout Greeks [probably proselytes to Judaism] and not a few of the leading women' (v. 4). Quiet persuasion, using the exposition of Old Testament texts to proclaim Jesus as Messiah, by means of explanation and proof was the methodology. In the synagogue at Berea, the same approach is used. 'They received the word with all eagerness, examining the Scriptures daily to see if these things were so' (Acts 17:11). Again, Luke's comment is pertinent. He continues, 'Many of them therefore believed...' (v. 12). Because 'faith comes from hearing, and hearing through the word of Christ' (Rom. 10:17), Luke expects the declaration of Christ in all the Scriptures to produce believers and in the next verse describes this activity as proclaiming the Word of God (v. 13). So wherever, the Scriptures are accepted and available they are opened and expounded as the foundation documents for the apostolic preaching.

But what about Athens, that city 'full of idols'? There is a very significant verse at the start of Luke's account. Paul 'reasoned in the synagogue with the Jews and the devout persons (proselytes)', just as he had in the other cities, but then Luke adds, 'and in the market-place every day with those who happened to be there' (Acts 17:17). This is what brought him the opportunity to explain his 'new teaching' in the forum of the Areopagus. What is interesting is that he reasoned his case with both those who had the Scriptures and those who knew nothing about them. The Areopagus address, which follows, indicates just how that worked. Paul's method is expository, even without the common ground of the open Scriptures. It has often been recognised that his strategy was to undermine and deconstruct the false religion of the worship of the 'unknown God'. His exposition is built on three negatives, each of which is used to expound the content of the Old Testament revelation. Let's see how it worked.

Firstly, he declares that God 'does not live in temples made by man'. Behind this assertion is the teaching about creation straight from Genesis, that He is 'the God who made the world and everything in it, being Lord of heaven and earth' (v. 24). Far from needing a temple to dwell in He has created the world for us to dwell in. The second negative follows. 'Nor is he served by human hands, as though he needed anything.' This declaration is supported by the Biblical truth that the universe and all human life is sustained by its creator, 'since he himself gives to all mankind life and breath and everything' (v. 25). He doesn't need us, but all that we have depends on him. The final negative is that God is not remote and unknowable, since 'he is actually not far from each one of us' (v. 27). And as his lead-up to this point, Paul adduces the Biblical teaching that 'he made from one man every nation of mankind' (v. 26) with the purpose that 'they should seek God' since we are his offspring (v. 27-28).

Having demolished the inability of any idolatry, basing his argument on the clear self-revelation of God in the Old Testament Scriptures (v. 29) he is then in a position to declare the difference that now exists since God has called all people everywhere to repent and confirmed His coming judgement of all humanity, through a man whom He has appointed, 'by raising him from the dead' (v. 31). Christ, the centre of all the Scriptures, risen, ascended, glorified and coming to judge, is the focus of His message but the route there is provided by the exposition of Biblical revelation.

Moving on to Corinth, the familiar pattern is repeated. 'He reasoned in the synagogue every Sabbath, and tried to persuade (that verb again) Jews and Greeks' (18:4). The synagogue ruler, Crispus, believed in the Lord and 'many of the Corinthians hearing Paul believed and were baptized' (v. 8). But what did they continue to hear as the infant church in Corinth was planted and grew? Luke's summary is instructive. 'And he (Paul) stayed a year and six months, teaching the word of God among them' (v. 11). Eighteen months of Biblical expository teaching was what provided solid foundations for this church in a famously amoral city.

Finally, Paul moves from Greece to the province of Asia and arrives at Ephesus, where typically he 'reasoned with the Jews' in the synagogue (Acts 18:19). Returning later, 'he entered the synagogue and for three months spoke boldly, reasoning and persuading them about the kingdom of God' (Acts 19:8). Meeting resistance he withdrew and 'took the disciples with him, reasoning daily in the hall of Tyrannus. This continued for two years, so that all the residents of Asia heard the word of the Lord, both Jews and Greeks.' (vv. 9-10). Whatever their background, whether they knew the Scriptures or not, the exposition of their content, focussed on Christ as their fulfilment, seems invariably to have been the apostolic practice.

By way of summary, Luke records for us Paul's farewell address to the Ephesian elders a chapter later, where he reminds them of the record of his ministry among them, which as far as we know was his longest period of settled ministry. He identifies it as three years (Acts 20:31). It is the verbs that Paul uses which are so instructive. 'Declaring and teaching' (v. 20), 'testifying' (vv. 21, 24), 'proclaiming the Kingdom' (v. 25), 'declaring the whole counsel of God' (v. 27), 'admonishing everyone with tears' ('v. 31). This was all word ministry, rooted in the Scriptures, explaining and expounding their meaning. This was what built the young churches of the apostolic era. And that is why Paul's parting blessing, to those whom he has charged to care for the flock in Ephesus, is entirely in terms of their word ministry. 'And now I commend you to God and to the word of his grace, which is able to build you up and to give you the inheritance among all those who are sanctified' (Acts 20:32). The same Word that generates faith builds the church and sanctifies its members. Because there is no alternative plan (how could one be needed?), the entire apostolic ministry rests on the proclamation of Christ, through the exposition of God's Word.

## Building the Church on the Scripture

Another major strand, supporting the centrality of exposition, is provided by the many examples of the use of Scripture in the epistles. This is obviously a huge subject, but it is striking how often the theological and ethical arguments and exhortations of the New Testament rely upon, expand and explain Old Testament scriptures. Clearly, all of the apostles understood the Old Testament Christologically, as Jesus Himself taught them (Luke 24:27, 44-47). Sometimes they began with the fact of the Messiahship of Jesus, validated by His resurrection, and using their own experience of Christ as Lord worked back to a proper understanding of the Scriptures' purpose and fulfilment. But often Paul seems to work from his understanding of the Old Testament text, in its context, and move from there to the person and work of Christ.

Sometimes the whole new covenant teaching hangs on the exposition of key statements in the Old Testament text. Galatians 3:7-9 provides a prime example of this. In undermining the false teaching of the 'troublers', who are invading the churches with their insistence on the works of the law, Paul uses two great Genesis statements. 'Abraham believed God, and it was counted to him as righteousness' (Gen. 15:6) and the earlier covenant promise, 'In you shall all the nations be blessed' (Gen. 12:3). Between the two quotations the apostle expounds their significance for his readers—he unpacks their meaning. Those of faith are the sons of Abraham, irrespective of ethnicity, and the promise to Abraham was a preaching of the good news 'before-hand', namely that God would justify the Gentiles by faith.

As the chapter proceeds and the argument develops, verses 10-13 each contain a Scriptural quotation from the Old Testament, which Paul expounds to clinch his point. He is not proof-texting, but expounding the Christological significance of each verse. Humanity is under God's curse due to lawlessness. The impossibility of sinful human beings ever being able to keep the law means that another means of justification has to be provided and that is through faith in the redemptive work of God's Messiah. The exposition of verses from Deuteronomy, Habakkuk and Leviticus is how Paul argues for and teaches the fundamental principles of the new covenant.

Sometimes, it is the exposition of one word in the Old Testament text that is used to make the New Testament point with unquestionable authority. So, a few verses later, Paul writes, 'Now the promises were made to Abraham and to his offspring. It does not say 'And to offsprings', referring to many, but referring to one, 'And to your offspring', who is Christ.' (Gal. 3:16). Taking the detail of Scripture seriously requires expository method in the teaching.

The same implication is true if we believe that the Scriptures, old and new, are integral parts of the one united divine self-revelation, so that Scripture interprets Scripture, as one harmonious whole. The nature of cumulative revelation is that the later texts illuminate and expound the earlier, not because the earlier revelation is in any way deficient, but because the light is shining with increasing clarity and penetration until it comes to its full radiance in the person of Jesus Christ. We can take an example as evidence of this normal methodology by linking together three passages from very different times in salvation history, which refer to the same historical incident.

## Old and New Testaments Working Together

Exodus 17:1-7 is the account of the divine provision of water from the rock at Rephidim, when Moses struck it with the rod of God. It is economic in its detail, but more than a merely narrative account there is also a clear message being expounded in the two names which Moses gives to the place—Massah (testing) and Meribah (quarrelling) 'because they tested the LORD by saying, "Is the LORD among us or not?"' (Exod. 17:7). It is historically true, sobering in its message, but there is more light to break forth centuries later, as the writer of Psalm 95 increases our understanding. The fresh revelation here is that the testing and quarrelling arose from hardening of the heart (Ps. 95:8). The culpability of Israel is increased by the disclosure that they tested God 'though they had seen my work' (v. 9). We may think of the plagues, the Passover, the Red Sea, and the manna. The diagnosis deepens. 'They are a people who go astray in their heart, and they have not known my ways' (v. 10). Exposition like this does not take us through the Exodus account, as it were, verse by verse, but it picks up the clues of Massah and Meribah in order to shine more light from its own later perspective on the earlier text.

How much more is this the case in the New Testament! Hebrews 3 provides us with one of the clearest and most powerful Biblical examples of a Christian expositor dealing with a Scripture text. That text is printed out for us in Hebrews 3:7-11, which is an exact quotation of Psalm 95:7-11. There is the passage up front for us all to hear before the expositor gets to work on it. His exposition runs from 3:12 right through to 4:13. Beginning with a sobering warning, 'Take care, brothers ....' He traces the rebellion of Exodus 17 and Psalm 95 to 'an evil, unbelieving heart', not to the circumstances of their thirst but to their rebellious reaction, which he describes as 'being hardened by the deceitfulness of sin' (v. 13). That phrase invites the contemporary expositor to explore how sin never produces the 'good' that temptation promises, but that its indulgence results in the accumulation of increasing layers of hardness in the heart towards God.

As the danger is exposed, the urgency of action is stressed as the preacher highlights the word 'Today' in the Psalm's text. Every time God's voice is heard there is a choice to be made of obedience or rebellion. Each 'today' is of immense importance because there is an end, to which we are progressing. The generation that experienced the grace of God in the exodus never entered the promised land and the Hebrews text expounds the reasons why. They heard and yet rebelled (v. 16). They provoked God's wrath by their sin (v. 17). The essence of that sin was disobedience (v. 18) and the root of their tragic demise was unbelief (v. 18). That was why they put God to the test. They heard the message of good news; think of the covenant promises at Sinai. But they did not respond with faith; they did not really listen (4:2). The preacher then relates all this directly to his hearers as he returns to his opening theme. We too have the promise of entering God's Sabbath rest, ceasing from reliance on our works to put our faith in Christ. The original readers of the letter were being tempted to go back to Judaism, to their pre-Christian experience and lifestyle, but the message of the letter is that there is nothing to go back to. Jesus is the only way to God. 'Therefore, while the promise of entering his rest still stands, let us fear lest any of you should seem to have failed to reach it' (4:1). Everything will depend on what his readers do with the living and active Word of God (4:12) which they have just heard expounded.

We can see from these and many other Biblical examples that the preachers of Scripture, in Scripture, are text driven and see their responsibility not only to state and explain its meaning, but also to apply its continuing relevance to their own hearers. They want to expose its significance. Even the introduction to the Psalm 95 quotation in Hebrews 3:7 makes that clear, since the verse starts, 'Therefore, as the Holy Spirit says', or 'is saying'. That centuries-old psalm is the living, enduring, active Word of God, both to the first and twenty-first century readers. And that is the consistent attitude and conviction of all the New Testament authors. But we must not narrow that in our own thinking to a wooden scholastic commentary on the text and call the laying out of our textual exegesis an 'expository' sermon.

Richard N. Longenecker makes the point well in his 1999 Eerdmans title *Biblical Exegesis in the Apostolic Period* (p. 191). He comments, 'What we have in the preaching and writings of the early apostolic band indicates that the apostles were not so much interested in commentaries on the biblical texts or the application of principles to issues of the day as they were in demonstrating redemptive fulfilment in Jesus of Nazareth. Accepting the messiahship and lordship of Jesus, and believing that in his teaching and person was expressed the fullness of divine revelation, they took a prophetic stance on a revelatory basis and treated the Old Testament more charismatically than scholastically.' In other words, they were preachers, not merely exegetes. Scripture itself bears eloquent witness to the purpose of the divine self-revelation always being ultimately personal and relational. God does not speak simply to convey accurate authoritative information about Himself, though Scripture always does that, but to change human lives, to command all people everywhere to repent, to testify about repentance toward God and faith in our Lord Jesus Christ.

If we are convinced about the centrality of this Biblical expository approach to the Scriptures, how can we ensure that it impacts, shapes and energises our own preaching ministry? Let me suggest that there are four steps we need to take in preparing our expository sermon. Over the years, I have found that having this template in my mind whenever I come to prepare has been an invaluable aid to keep me on track and to keep me persevering in this good and vital work.

## Essential Steps in Preparation

Step 1 – We begin with the exegesis of the passage. Here the secret is to assume nothing, however well you think you know the text. Listen carefully to what this text actually says, not what you think it might say, or what you would like it to say. Grapple with the text so that you understand its plain meaning as fully as you can. This will involve attention to the vocabulary, why the words are selected and how they function in the structure of the sentences or the unit. Obviously, the different genres of the Bible will require differing techniques in doing this. Hebrew poetry does not work the same way as a Pauline theological argument. I find it helpful to look for the surprises in my reading of the text as they often help me to dig a little further beneath the surface. Above all I need to read, read and read again, perhaps in more than one translation, so as to immerse my mind in it. However, it will soon begin to affect my heart, to challenge me in the control centre of my personality. Will my heart harden or soften? I cannot preach to others from my heart to theirs unless my heart is responsive to the message. My aim through this period of exegetical study is to be able to express the meaning of the passage and to attempt to summarise its essential message in a theme sentence, which expresses what I must preach if I am to be faithful to the text.

Step 2 – My next study period is geared to the exposition of the text, as I explore what the meaning signifies. Some preachers call this the pastoral intention of the text – why it is where it is and what it is designed to achieve. There is some detective work to be done here, exploring the contexts of the passage, both in its immediate setting (what immediately precedes and what follows it) and in its whole book setting. How does this section relate to the bigger picture of the whole book, its theme tune or melodic line? Of course, there is an even wider and richer context, which is the whole Bible, so it is important to be thinking about where this passage fits in the whole scope of salvation-history and in relation to God's biggest picture of all, from creation to the new creation. This is especially important when we are preaching from the Old Testament. What contribution does this passage make to the whole sweep of Biblical theology?

Looking at the passage through these lenses inevitably leads us towards its application. Rather than importing things we want to say, from our framework, we want to explore the concerns of the writer and to track the implications of the text before us. This is answering the 'so what?' questions. It is often the context study that gives the expositor the clues he needs to apply the passage well. That will come when we are cutting with the grain of the wood, tapping in to what the original purpose was, understanding why he says what he says. When we see not only the content but its implications for the original readers, as much as we can, we are able to determine not just what we are going to preach, but why we are going to preach it. This moves us on from exegetical lecturing to expository preaching. When this work is done it is helpful to sum up the purpose and direction of the emerging sermon in an aim sentence. Not only does this articulate the reason for the sermon's existence, but it also becomes the focus of my prayers. This is what I am asking the Lord graciously to do through my preaching of this text. He will, of course, do whatever He sovereignly wills. No one can predict all the outcomes of a faithful exposition; but it is very likely that if we are seeking the text's original purpose to be fulfilled in our very different contemporary context that is what the Holy Spirit will achieve. Those who aim at nothing are usually likely to hit it.

There are two further stages in the expository process to which we need to devote considerable time in our preparation. These are working on the structure and strategy for the sermon (Step 3) and then, finally, producing whatever notes we need (Step 4).

Step 3 – The theme and aim sentences need to be constantly in mind as we work at how to present the passage to our hearers. The shape of the passage will usually dictate the shape of the sermon and a sequential journey through the text is a great benefit in engaging and keeping the hearers' attention. Though we have spent time mulling over the text and its implications most of our hearers will not, so we need to provide them with a map for the journey, build bridges for connection between the text and our context and help them to see the value of the time we are spending together in the Scripture. Headings or summary sentences are really important as the sermon develops, to aid understanding and memorability. But it is equally important to show how the applications derive from the text itself and what they may look like in life today, which is where illustration can play a vital part.

Step 4 – Note writing is a very personal skill. Good notes are whatever helps the expositor to preach with confidence and clarity, faithfully and effectively, cutting a straight furrow with the word of truth. They may be detailed or brief, a full script or just some key headings, but whatever the end product this last stage in the process is the time to choose the most effective vocabulary, sentence structure and division of time to present the message with clarity and power. All this requires not only hard work, but prayer, prayer and more prayer throughout the entire preparation process. For 'neither he who plants nor he who waters is anything, but only God who gives the growth' (1 Cor. 3:7). 'Unless the Lord builds the house, those who build it labour in vain.' (Ps. 127:1) 'I am the vine; you are the branches. Whoever abides in me and I in him, he it is that bears much fruit, for apart from me you can do nothing.' (John 15:5) Not very little, but nothing! These are verses to have before every would-be expositor in our preparation time because they will drive us over and over again to turn to the Lord in prayer, for understanding, wisdom, clarity and effectiveness. 'Let him who has my word speak my word faithfully. What has straw in common with wheat? declares the LORD. Is not my word like fire, declares the LORD, and like a hammer that breaks the rock in pieces?' (Jer. 23:28-29).

As John Chapman used to say, 'There's more than one way of skinning a cat' and there's certainly more than one way of preparing an expository talk or sermon. We shall develop the processes that help us best, but I suspect that in some way or other they will each involve the disciplines we have been outlining, if they are to achieve the desired end. Just as in the study we covet that eye-opening moment, when the text suddenly comes alive and we say to ourselves, 'Oh, now I see; that is what it means!'— so through prayer and hard work we long that our preached exposition will produce the same illumination for our hearers. Jesus breaks the bread and we distribute it to his hungry followers. However, sometimes there is a resistance, even a rejection of what God is saying. Particularly in congregations unused to exposition, there can be a strong reaction to the plainness of Scripture with its stark choices and life-changing imperatives. Rather than hungry sheep, the appropriate analogy might seem to be a radar screen set to neutralise incoming missiles. 'Today if you hear his voice, do not harden your hearts.' But whatever the reaction, the expositor has God's Word and he has his knees and he must go on faithfully using both, because his confidence is that the Word of God in the hands of the Spirit of God will always accomplish the work of God, whether in salvation or judgement.

He will constantly return to Paul's charge to pastor Timothy in Ephesus as if it were directly to his own soul. 'Preach the word; be ready in season and out of season;

reprove, rebuke, and exhort, with complete patience and teaching. For the time is coming when people will not endure sound teaching, but having itching ears they will accumulate for themselves teachers to suit their own passions, and will turn away from listening to the truth and wander off into myths. As for you, always be sober-minded, endure suffering, do the work of an evangelist, fulfil your ministry.' (2 Tim. 4:2-5) There can be no greater challenge and no greater Biblical mandate for expository preaching.

# 4
## TWO EXPOSITORY EXAMPLES

I was asked to provide some examples of my 'Essential Steps in Preparation', which I do below. Of course, what follows is nothing more than a personal and very sketchy summary of hours of preparation.

### 1 Peter 2:4-12

[4]As you come to him, a living stone rejected by men but in the sight of God chosen and precious, [5]you yourselves like living stones are being built up as a spiritual house, to be a holy priesthood, to offer spiritual sacrifices acceptable to God through Jesus Christ. [6]For it stands in Scripture:

> 'Behold, I am laying in Zion a stone, a cornerstone chosen and precious, and whoever believes in him will not be put to shame.'

[7]So the honour is for you who believe, but for those who do not believe,

> 'The stone that the builders rejected has become the cornerstone,'

[8]and

> 'A stone of stumbling,
> and a rock of offence.'

They stumble because they disobey the word, as they were destined to do.

⁹But you are a chosen race, a royal priesthood, a holy nation, a people for his own possession, that you may proclaim the excellencies of him who called you out of darkness into his marvellous light. ¹⁰Once you were not a people, but now you are God's people; once you had not received mercy, but now you have received mercy.

¹¹Beloved, I urge you as sojourners and exiles to abstain from the passions of the flesh, which wage war against your soul. Keep your conduct among the Gentiles honourable, so that when they speak against you as evildoers, they may see your good deeds and glorify God on the day of visitation.

### Step One
### Exegesis: Observations and Questions

Note the preceding section has focussed on new birth through the Gospel which is all about Christ (1:19-21).

V. 4   He is the one to whom 'you come'. 'Living stone' is a vivid image, repeated in v. 5 about 'you'. The contrast is about human rejection and divine choice (a difference already noted in 1:1-2).

V. 5   Two metaphors – house and priesthood (temple resonances). What are the 'Spiritual sacrifices' Christians offer?

V. 6   Quotation from Isaiah 28:16. Study in context. Judah is being tempted to look to Egypt (of all places!) for deliverance from the Assyrians. 'Put to shame' has the idea of running away at speed. Trust Egypt rather than Yahweh and that is what will happen.

V. 7   'Honour' contrasts with shame (v. 6). Faith contrasts with unbelief. The quote from Psalm 118:22 echoes the 'rejection' idea in v. 4 and shows how futile it is.

V. 8   The third Old Testament quote in Isaiah 8:14 contrasts God as the stumbling stone through unbelief with God as sanctuary to the believer. Note how disobedience is the product of unbelief.

V. 9   Echoes of Exodus 19:6, establishing the redeemed Israel's covenant identity. Parallels? 'So that' – important for understanding God's purpose and our obligations. Contrast darkness and light.

V. 10 Two further contrasts, marking out God's distinctively different people from the world. Echoes of Hosea 1:6-11. God's purpose for His people.

V. 11 Relationship to world, demanding appropriate conduct.

V. 12 In the world, but different from it. Gentiles = nations. Echoes of Matthew 5:15. What is the 'day of visitation'?

*Theme Sentence: Believers are to live distinctively good lives in the Christ-rejecting world, to proclaim God's glory.*

## Step Two
### Exposition: Significance and Purpose
Why is Peter so concerned for his readers to 'live such good lives among the pagans'? Consider: the fulfilment of God's salvation plan in the creation of the new covenant community (vv. 4-5), the glory brought to God when this

new people (v. 10) live holy and good lives in spite of the darkness and hostility (v. 9-12).

Consider this passage in terms of the book context:

- The 'various trials' they are suffering (1:6), their sense of exile and alienation (1:1-2).

- The contrast between their old way of life in the world (1:14, 18) and the new (1:22-23) – note the three contrasts in 2:9-10.

- The calling theme (key to v. 9) in the rest of the letter – see 1:15-16, 2:20-21, 3:9, 5:10.

Emphasis is on the central reason for the distinctiveness, which is not moral goodness, but coming to Christ. Everything revolves around the idea of living stones being built together on Christ, the precious Cornerstone, to form a new temple, in which God's glory ('excellencies' v. 9) is displayed, as the builder. Need to stress the inevitability of this God-given different identity, as is later developed in 4:12-13. Note the repeats 'Once...but now' (v. 10). Note also the two practical applications which follow – imperatives in verses 11 & 12.

Verses 11-12 not only contain imperatives, but provide help on how to fulfil them. We are to accept our existence in the world as 'sojourners and exiles'. We are not at home. Our citizenship is elsewhere.

Verses 5 and 9, which are expounding the great privileges of being God's chosen people, united to His chosen and precious Son, to stimulate our gratitude for God's grace and motivates us to live accordingly.

The 'day of visitation' is a difficult phrase. It could mean the day of judgement, but it is hard to see how the present good deeds of believers will lead unbelievers to glorify God, when every knee must bow. Calvin's view is more convincing – that the good deeds of believers are used to prepare for the day when Christ visits an individual's life with saving and transforming power (e.g. Zacchaeus). See the same vocabulary in Luke 19:43-44.

*Aim sentence: Be active in glorifying God by living as his holy people, even though this may provoke hostility, because your identity is in Christ.*

### Step Three
### Structure and strategy: Outline and Applications
What is it that will prevent us from living according to the teaching of this passage? Fear of men (too great a cost)? The isolation which it will produce? 'The passions of the flesh' (v. 11) inclining us to compromise rather than confrontation?

How can the positive teaching come across so as to motivate us to follow Peter's urging us to live as 'exiles' – in the world, but distinct from it?

Divide the passage into three sections and use the contrast which runs all the way through as the unifying subtext in all of the three headings. The distinction is God-given, through the new birth, but accepting it is crucial to all that follows. It leads to a different mind-set (perspective) which will transform both attitudes and life-style. This, in turn, is essential if the Gospel is to go on spreading and unbelievers are to be brought to glorify

God and be built up into God's 'spiritual house', His new covenant people.

Explore Biblical examples, those from church history and from life today that illustrate and anchor the main teaching.

In the introduction, establish the common contemporary problem of widespread loneliness, but see that Christians experience a particular type of cultural alienation (exile). Emphasise the need to have a truly Biblical view of this dilemma, but reflecting on extremes of identity or withdrawal in church history. Not a pendulum swing but a Biblical plumbline is what is needed.

Work out how much Old Testament reference to include, as it could be overwhelming. It is probably better to go for one reference in some detail than cover them all too briefly.

As verse 12 is in many ways the key verse to the whole section, the sermon needs to develop a clear flow of ideas through the passage, to give momentum to the urgent appeal at the end.

### Step Four
### Write Sermon Notes

The full script for this sermon is included as Appendix 1 (on page 79).

As a further addendum, it has been suggested that it might be helpful to provide some jottings to illustrate the preparation process for an Old Testament passage. Again, these will necessarily be brief, but may give some idea of ways of possible approach.

## Isaiah 6:1-13
## 'THE HOLY ONE OF ISRAEL'

[1]In the year that King Uzziah died I saw the Lord sitting upon a throne, high and lifted up; and the train of his robe filled the temple. [2]Above him stood the seraphim. Each had six wings: with two he covered his face, and with two he covered his feet, and with two he flew. [3]And one called to another and said:

> 'Holy, holy, holy is the Lord of hosts; the whole earth
> is full of his glory!'

[4]And the foundations of the thresholds shook at the voice of him who called, and the house was filled with smoke. [5]And I said: 'Woe is me! For I am lost; for I am a man of unclean lips, and I dwell in the midst of a people of unclean lips; for my eyes have seen the King, the Lord of hosts!'

[6]Then one of the seraphim flew to me, having in his hand a burning coal that he had taken with tongs from the altar. And he touched my mouth and said: 'Behold, this has touched your lips; your guilt is taken away, and your sin atoned for.'

[8]And I heard the voice of the Lord saying, 'Whom shall I send, and who will go for us?' Then I said, 'Here I am! Send me.' [9]And he said, 'Go, and say to this people:

> "Keep on hearing, but do not understand; keep on
> seeing, but do not perceive."

[10]Make the heart of this people dull, and their ears heavy, and blind their eyes; lest they see with their

eyes, and hear with their ears, and understand with
their hearts, and turn and be healed.'

¹¹Then I said, 'How long, O Lord?' And he said:
'Until cities lie waste without inhabitant, and houses
without people, and the land is a desolate waste,
¹²and the Lord removes people far away, and
the forsaken places are many in the midst of the
land. ¹³And though a tenth remain in it, it will be
burned again, like a terebinth or an oak, whose
stump remains when it is felled. The holy seed is its
stump.'

### Step One
### Exegesis: Observations and Quotations

V. 1   King Uzziah reigned 792-740 B.C., the last eight
years as a leper (2 Chron. 26). The end of an era of
great prosperity. But chapter 5 has already shown us the
condition of God's vineyard. Isaiah's call comes through
this vision of the true King, the Holy One of Israel. The
temple can only house the outskirts of His robe.

V. 2   Seraphim means 'the burning ones' (fire and light
motif).

V. 3   Three times 'holy' is the superlative form of the
adjective. Lord = Yahweh (think covenant!) hosts = armies.
Holiness is the essence of the divine nature and the whole
earth is the theatre for the display of his glory.

V. 4   Earthquake and fire – echoes of Sinai (Exod. 19).

V. 5   Overwhelming sense of sin is always the conse-
quence of encounter with God. Compare N.T. expan-

sions in John 12:40-41 (quoting Isa. 6:10) and v. 45.
2 Corinthians 4:6, John 1:14.

V. 6  The cleansing is not simply by fire but comes from
the altar of sacrifice.

V. 7  Applied especially to the area of conscious
sinfulness and confession.

V. 8  The one who was excluded is brought near to hear
God's call. The man who was silenced is sent to speak.

V. 9-10 Indicate that a ministry of Biblical proclamation
may harden and condemn as well as rescue.

V. 11-13 The response is entirely in God's hands and
Isaiah's ministry will focus on the coming judgement in the
exile, but also on the promise of the holy seed in the stump
(see 11:1-3).

*Theme Sentence: The Holy One of Israel constantly
reveals His glory, both in His cleansing power and through
His righteous judgement, so that there is always hope.*

## Step Two
### Exposition: Significance and Purpose
Set the text in its contexts (1) Historical – the prosperity
of Uzziah's early reign led to pride and to his downfall.
Symbolic of all that was wrong in the nation. (2) Book
– why is the call narrative delayed until chapter 6?
The first five chapters outline the desperate condition of
Judah, but God lays hold of Isaiah to exemplify in his life
what he is willing to do for the nation. (3) Whole Bible.
Only the coming of the Messiah, his atoning death and
resurrection will be able to change self-willed, hardened

hearts to worship the Holy One of Israel (Israel's favourite title for God).

Explore the idea of holiness not only as a moral righteousness and purity, but as the utter 'otherness' of God, the essence of His being. Develop our consciousness that every inch of our planet is His and that all creation witnesses to His righteousness, power and compassion. Use John 12 to relate this to seeing God's glory in Christ.

Isaiah's conviction of sin uses the leper's (Uzziah's) cry 'Unclean'. The nearer we get to God, the more we shall realise the depravity of our own hearts. The three elements of Isaiah's call are conviction, confession, followed by cleansing (1 John 1:8-9 parallel). God's cleansing, re-storing and renewing work is also the revelation of His glory. (Parallels in John to Christ being 'glorified' or 'lifted up'). Then the commissioning can follow (v. 9).

But in human terms the call is to be a failure; the message will largely be rejected, though a small remnant is gathered (ch. 8). See verses 11-13 and Isaiah 11:1-3.

Practical applications to include that we have to become humbled sinners before we can be commissioned servants. It is often when things are at their darkest that God's new beginnings occur. There is always more grace.

*Aim Sentence: Trust God to fulfil His purposes in our generation. As believers we need to humble ourselves before His holiness, seek His continuing cleansing and commit our lives to His service.*

## Step Three
## Structure and Strategy: Outline and Applications

The passage divides into two major sections, God's dealing with Isaiah (vv. 1-7) and then God's commissioning to his prophetic ministry (vv. 8-13).

There is an emphasis on the newness of God's intervention here, against the dark background of Judah's faithlessness. So it might be good to import that into the headings, which might be (1) A New Vision of the Holy One (vv. 1-4), (2) A New Realisation of Sin (vv. 5-7) and (3) A New Focus of Service (vv. 8-13).

In the introduction some general parallels between the state of God's people in Judah and the low condition of the contemporary church can be drawn, because the chastening discipline of the Lord is a constant response to the self-willed pride and disobedience of the covenant community.

We are not Isaiah and we are not given his task, but we do need Isaiah's convictions if we are to be faithful servants and these come from his overwhelming vision of God's holiness and him casting himself on God's mercy. When we see His holiness (glory revealed in Christ) and our own abject failure and sin, there is no room for pride. The only response is a life lived every day at the cross in repentance and faith and every day amazed at, and totally dependent on, the Holy One of Israel.

The narrative guards against any presumption that faithful service will always produce fruit. Doubtless Isaiah would have longed to see a national revival, but that was not God's plan. Instead, he was called to explain the coming dark days of judgement, but beyond the exile to point to the hope of the holy seed in the coming of the Christ. What God primarily required from Isaiah (and us) was faithfulness, obedience to His will. Whether spiritual understanding is the fruit of faithful witness, or not, is God's prerogative. A passage like this should challenge all our ideas about successful churches and how they can be created, replacing our small ambitions with a vision of the holiness of God, who orders everything according to His perfect will. The greatest contribution we can make to God's service is our personal holiness.

# APPENDIX 1

This sermon is re-worked from notes of a preached exposition which I gave as part of a consecutive series working through the first letter of Peter. In the course of that series I came to regard the exhortation at the start of verse 12 as something of a strapline for the whole epistle. Unfortunately, the ESV translation, 'Keep your conduct among the Gentiles honourable', while accurate is somewhat leaden-footed, even a little opaque. I much prefer the NIV's, 'Live such good lives among the pagans ....' and so chose that as my overall title for the exposition. I have tried to keep the sermon that follows as near to the spoken word as possible.

## 'Good Lives Among the Pagans'

One of life's challenging experiences is the feeling that you don't belong. You enter a crowded room, but you don't recognise anybody you know. You go to a new church and stay around for a coffee at the end, but everyone is in their own clique and nobody speaks to you. It's an unnerving situation. It's as though you don't really exist, or are not worth bothering with. God made us for relationships, so to feel 'shut out' is demoralising, although a recent survey by the British Red Cross came up with the startling information that more than 9 million people in the U.K., across all adult age groups, see themselves as either always or often lonely. That's a figure about the size of the population of London.

Loneliness may be one of the inescapable facts of modern life, but how we navigate it will have profound effects on our mental and physical health. Yet for Christians the experience of not belonging to our culture, suffering exclusion and rejection, is normal. That doesn't make it any easier to deal with, and the way we navigate its challenges will have profound effects on our spiritual health. It may be expressed in its extreme forms through physical persecution, imprisonment, torture, even martyrdom, or more often in its subtle hostility of social ostracism, mockery, and discrimination, generating anxiety, instability and fear. The relationship of the Christian believer, whether individual or corporate, to the unbelieving world is one of the most important and pressingly urgent issues to settle, whether in Peter's day or our own.

As we have already seen, this letter is written to marginalised and suffering churches, across the land mass we call Turkey, along the southern coast of the Black Sea close to the Iranian border. They were scattered groups of isolated believers across a wide area, 'elect exiles of the dispersion' (1:1). Not only were they scattered but being 'grieved by various trials' (1:6). Viewed by their neighbours with puzzlement, sometimes resentment and open hostility, they were increasingly pursued by the Roman imperial cult as atheists, because they worshipped no visible gods and refused to confess that Caesar is Lord. Their spiritual wellbeing as well as the future progress of the gospel depended on a mature perspective and godly reaction to this dilemma.

It has been the same down the centuries ever since. A survey of church history over the two millennia soon reveals a swing of the pendulum by way of response. Sometimes the church has withdrawn from the hostile world into a fortress-mentality ghetto, a tightly defined community of the faithful, seeking to cultivate holiness in an hermetically-sealed environment. At other times, the church has advanced into the world, adapting the social norms, affirming the culture and on occasions even baptising it. The one can be a reaction against the other, as the times change and the pendulum swings. Both extremes have their advantages and weaknesses and doubtless each makes its appeal to different temperaments. But those who withdraw would do well to remember Martin Luther's warning that it is one thing to take the monk out of the world, but quite another to take the world out of the monk! And the world affirmers need to recognise that sitting where they sit has so often led to being what they are, until, through accommodation and compromise, the church becomes indistinguishable from the world.

When the pendulum swings the answer is not to counter-balance it by pressure in the opposite direction, but to ask where is the Biblical perpendicular and then to seek to settle God's people on the plumb-line of God's Word. That is Peter's concern here in the letter and I trust it will be yours personally and ours corporately as we sit under his teaching. Note firstly what he draws our attention towards.

## 1. A Crucial Distinction (vv. 4-8)

It is the distinction between the church and the world, which runs all the way through our verses: the inescapable fact that the people who belong to God and those who do not are as different as chalk from cheese! The Gentiles (or pagans) in verse 12 translates literally as 'the nations'. It's the customary Old Testament distinction between Israel and all the other people groups, those within the covenant and those not. We are to live among them, taking our full part as reliable members of whatever communities we belong to, but we are to live distinctively different lives ('such good lives' v. 12). The important point to understand is what creates that distinction.

It is not natural goodness that marks out the believer. We are constantly being told how many fine people there are in the world, who do a great deal of good, but who are not Christians. At a human level that is true because God's common grace operates in every society as a restraint so that the unbelieving world is never as bad as it could be. But that is not the distinction. That is found at the start of verse 4. What marks the Christian out from the nations is that 'you came to him', Christ the Lord. And you came to Him as the living stone, the living divine person who is the foundation of the whole edifice we call the church. Christ is the living stone and those who come to Him are described also in verse 5 as 'living stones'. The church is not a building or an institution or anything created by men.

It is a living organism brought into life by God Himself and by God alone.

The great divide in humanity is caused by an individual's attitude to Jesus Christ. As you read the verses, it could hardly be spelt out more clearly. What characterises the nations, referred to in verse 4 as 'men', is their rejection of Christ. The cross is the indisputable evidence of that fact. Verse 7 describes the world as 'those who do not believe', so that the person and claims of Christ become for them 'a stone of stumbling and a rock of offence' (v. 8a). Their defining characteristic is that 'they disobey the word' (v. 8b). This is not unbelief that longs to find faith. This is a determined refusal to come to Christ in repentance and submission—a personal rebellion that may eventually harden into a destiny of judgement and eternal separation from God. That is the normal non-Christian life. It may not be grossly immoral or outwardly hostile; it may be quite pleasant and affable, just unbelieving (Jesus is not Lord) and so disobedient (I will not repent and believe).

The letter insists several times that we get this distinction clear, by recognising where we all were before we came to Christ. 1:14 speaks of 'the passions of your former ignorance'. 1:18 calls it 'the futile ways inherited from your forefathers'. This very section reminds us that we were 'called out of darkness' (2:9) and that we were 'not a people' (2:10)—we had no lasting identity. 4:3 sums up life before Christ as 'lawless idolatry'.

It is Christ who makes all the difference. You come to believe in him (v. 6 and 7) and on the basis of that relationship everything else is predicated. Because Peter's major point is that if you are united to this Christ, as living stones in the spiritual house He is building (v. 5), you will be treated as He was. If He was rejected, suffered and even died, then don't be surprised at what you suffer (see also 4:12-13). But if He was 'in the sight of God chosen and precious' (v. 4), then so are you. And if He was raised to life as the living stone, then so are His believing people (v. 5).

That identity is clearly established in verse 6, by Peter's quotation from Isaiah 28:16. In its context the prophecy was given when Judah was trying to forge an alliance with Egypt, to defend them against the Assyrians. It led to disaster. Egypt was a broken reed and because Judah rejected the Lord for one of the idolatrous nations they were shamed by defeat and conquest. They became Assyria's vassal, which is what you get when you choose an alternative foundation to the Lord. But the thrust of Isaiah's word is that when the Lord lays the foundation, 'whoever believes will not be in haste', will not have to run away in disarray or dismay. As verse 7 teaches, honour replaces shame for the believer, who is built as a living stone into Christ.

Look again at those wonderful certainties in verse 5. When you come to Christ, you become part of the household of God, the church which He is building and part of the holy priesthood, 'to offer spiritual sacrifices acceptable to God through Jesus Christ'. Lives of obedience and godly living among the pagans are spiritual sacrifices of praise and thanksgiving for the precious cornerstone, the fruit of gratitude for all that God has done for us, in

Christ. Both the temple and the priesthood have found their fulfilment in Christ, the living stone, and through Him we have access into God's presence, in active service. The acceptance of this radical God-given distinction is the foundation of security and stability for Christian living in an unbelieving world. We need to take it in and remind ourselves of its reality every day of our earthly lives. The passage moves on—from the crucial distinction between the church and the world to ....

## 2. A Transformed Perspective (vv. 9-10)

This is equally essential in order for the church to live in the world. If they, and we, are to persevere in godly living, Peter wants us to grasp who we truly are, in Christ. Verse 9 has an arresting beginning. 'But you...' What he will explain is that to regard Christ as the precious cornerstone laid in Zion, as the foundation and key to all God's purposes is to enter experientially into all the privileges God promised to His covenant people in the Old Testament. We need to see the church with God's eyes, to correct our distorted, reductionist perspective, conditioned by the pagan world. As the media regularly intones the death of the church and the hostile powers stoke the fires of opposition, physical, social and intellectual, God tells Peter's readers their true identity, who they really are. Read verse 9 again. Stop, take a deep breath and really take it in!

The chosen cornerstone is the foundation of a chosen people. Although He was despised and rejected, He has been raised in glory and power, because He is Himself the heart of God's eternal plan. And so, through faith, is that little house church in Pontus or Bithynia, however hostile the local magistrates may be. The language of verse 9 is almost identical with that spoken to Israel in Exodus 19:6, 'You shall be to me a kingdom of priests and a holy nation.' The church is God's new Israel, His new covenant chosen people, His own treasured possession. In Christ the two offices of King and priest have been united. The prophetic picture of the priest-king, Melchizedek, has been fulfilled (Gen. 14:18) and the church is now the community of those who share both descriptions derivatively from our union with Christ. We are children of the King and we have privileged access into the holiest place of all. Further, the church is 'a holy nation', in the sense of being set apart for God's exclusive use as His personal possession. The word here in v. 9 is exactly the same as that translated as 'pagans' or 'Gentiles' in v. 12.

This new community created by God is unique in that it transcends all barriers of race, class, culture and gender; it is international in scope and eternal in duration. The very reason for its existence is to 'proclaim the excellencies of him' who created it for His own possession. There is a fine story from the later years of the Roman Empire when persecution against the Christians was particularly fierce. Church buildings had been erected by this time and in one town the Christian believers had taken shelter in their own church as a protection against the marauding soldiers. Sensing that there might be valuable artefacts in the building the persecutors tried to batter down the door, shouting 'Bring out your treasures!'. The door opened and the pastor gestured towards his gathered flock inside.

'These are God's treasures' was his calm response. Verse 10 makes the point with crystal clarity. Those scattered groups of believers are God's 'elect exiles', the new Israel, the people constituted by the mercy of God, in Jesus Christ. Whatever the pride of the hostile nations, the church is the only corporate community that has eternal identity and validity—the chosen people of the Living God. That is a transforming perspective.

It also carries with its privilege a strong sense of responsibility. As with Israel at the exodus, there can be no going back to Egypt, no return to the old life. But neither is there any need to fear, whatever threats the enemy may pose, since God is in sovereign control. Nor is there any fear of God's wrath and judgement, since He has called us out of darkness and 'into his marvellous light'. As believers we are never to be triumphalist since we know what sinners we are, but neither are we to be defeatist. We need to hold on to this transformed perspective, to remember all that has been achieved for us in Christ's death and resurrection and to let God's Word teach us our true identity in Jesus. Then we shall not fear for the future of the church, but be ready to accept the final important truth that Peter sets before us.

## 3. An Urgent Responsibility (vv. 11-12)

These verses deal with the impact the church is to have upon the world. It has already been flagged up at the end of verse 9. Why has God called us into this privileged relationship? To belong to Him, yes, but also to proclaim His excellencies, His mighty deeds. That is how we truly praise Him. Again, Peter is using Exodus language. The mighty deeds are the saving acts of God on behalf of His people, which reveal His glorious character and summon our praises.

This is our calling, as the rest of the letter underlines on several occasions. In 1:15-16 it's a call to holiness. 'As he who *called* you is holy, you also be holy in all your conduct, since it is written, 'You shall be holy, for I am holy'.' In 2:20-21 it is a call to suffering. 'If when you do good and suffer for it you endure, this is a gracious thing in the sight of God. For to this you have been *called*, because Christ also suffered for you, leaving you an example, so that you might follow in his steps.' In 3:9 it is a call to blessing. 'Do not repay evil for evil or reviling for reviling, but on the contrary, bless, for to this you were *called*, that you may obtain a blessing.' And in 5:10 it is a call to eternal glory. 'And after you have suffered a little while, the God of all grace, who has *called* you to his eternal glory in Christ, will himself restore, confirm, strengthen and establish you.' All these are the consequences of God's saving activity in Christ, as we come to Him, in faith, trust and obedience.

So then, our urgent responsibility, whether individually or corporately, as God's dearly loved people, is to fulfil His call and by our words and our lives to proclaim His glory. That is how we are to glorify God. It's by living a daily life that is holy, distinctively different, bearing witness before the watching world and then seeking to use all the opportunities we have to explain the reason for the hope that is in us (3:15) and proclaim the good news of God's glorious grace.

All this brings us back to our original issue. How is the believer, how is the church to relate to the world in which we are set? Verses 11-12 are full of practical help for those who have embraced the crucial distinction and are seeking to live in the transformed perspective. We have to recognise that we are not to live as though this world is our permanent residence. We are temporary residents, but we are not yet at home. In that sense, we do not belong. Its values and customs are not ours. In accepting that great reality we are galvanised not to want to escape from the world, but to see that our heavenly citizenship must both inspire and dictate our earthly existence. We are to 'abstain from the passions of the flesh' (v. 11) because they make war against our true souls, our real identity. The world, the flesh and, behind them both, the devil will always be our implacable enemies. As sojourners and exiles we are to steer clear of its values, behaviour and lifestyles, which will do us no good and only compromise the gospel. Don't accept uncritically its views about work or wealth, or education and status, or sex and relationships. Apply the transformed perspective and follow the positives of verse 12.

Living as a Christian in the world, proclaiming God's mighty deeds, His glorious salvation, by life and lip is our calling. That may well expose us to all kinds of vilification. We shall be accused of arrogance, bigotry, intolerance. We may face persistent criticism, mockery, outright hostility. But the reaction of the nations must not stop the believer from living a good life (honourable conduct) in the world, among its people. The reason is that God's purposes are centrally involved. He is gathering a people to Himself and for Himself. He is building His spiritual house. Some of us were among the most determined opponents at one time, but an amazing change has happened to us, which is described in verse 12b.

We saw a good life being lived out to the glory of God and while we hated what it stood for and the guilt it engendered in us, part of us grudgingly admired what we saw and began to be drawn towards the light. Then, in God's wonderful providence, the day of visitation occurred. The Christ, whom that good Christian life reflected and glorified, came to knock on the door of our house. It was 'the day of visitation', the day He came to call and to save. It was the day when Zacchaeus came down from the sycamore tree and welcomed Jesus into his home and his life. In that same nineteenth chapter of Luke, Jesus uses this very same phrase to describe his own coming to the city of Jerusalem, to bring God's mercy and saving power, not his judgement. But as they despised, rejected and crucified Him, His Word can only be one of the coming judgement. 'For the days will come upon you, when your enemies will set up a barricade around you and surround you and hem you in on every side and tear you down to the ground, you and your children within you. And they will not leave one stone upon another in you, because you did not know the time of your visitation.' (Luke 19:43-44)

The ultimate day of universal judgement is yet to come, when God's people will finally be vindicated before the watching world and God will be glorified in His righteous wrath. But this is still a day of visitation, a day of opportunity, described by Calvin as 'the time when he unites us to himself', the day He comes to save. We never know in whose life our good deeds will be the precursor of the knock on the door, when Jesus comes to visit and to call another of His elect exiles out of the darkness into his wonderful light. So, don't give up! Recognise the crucial distinctive, embrace the transformed perspective and take up the urgent responsibility. That is how God's people are called to live in this world, that is how we are to declare His praises. That is why we are in the world, but not of it. That is why, though sometimes isolated, we are never alone. We are God's own possession. Keep on keeping on, living good lives among the pagans!

# APPENDIX 2

Just as Shakespeare writes in *The Merchant of Venice* that, 'All that glisters is not gold,' it is also true that everything that is called exposition is not exposition. There are many 'Expositional Imposters' that lurk in churches. At the end of this book, *Why Expository Preaching* we are including this article by Mike Gilbart-Smith, the pastor of Twynholm Baptist Church in London. It identifies twelve imposters that might masquerade as Expository Sermons.

It originally appeared at 9Marks.org and is reprinted here with permission:

## Expositional Imposters

Mark Dever rightly describes expositional preaching as 'preaching that takes for the point of a sermon the point of a particular passage of Scripture.'

However, I have heard (and preached!) sermons that intend to be expositional, yet fall somewhat short. Below are a dozen pitfalls: five that don't make the message of the passage the message of the sermon and thus abuse the text, five that fail to connect the text to the congregation, and two that fail to recognise that preaching is ultimately God's work.

None of these observations are original to me. Many I learned at Eden Baptist Church in Cambridge in the mid-

90s. Others I've picked up along the way. Since writing a similar article a few years ago, I've included some suggestions people made for additions. I'm sure you can think of others.

## Imposters that Fail to See the Text

### 1. The 'Unfounded Sermon': The Text Is Misunderstood

Here the preacher says things that may be true, but in no sense come from a correct interpretation of the passage. He is careless either with the *content* of the text (e.g. the sermon on 'production, prompting, and inspiration' from the NIV of 1 Thessalonians 1:3, though each word has no parallel in the Greek) or with the *context* (e.g. the sermon on David and Goliath, that asks 'who is your Goliath, and what are the five smooth stones that you need to be prepared to use against him?').

If a preacher is not deeply mining the truth of God's Word to determine the message of his sermons, they are likely being driven by his own ideas not God's.

### 2. The 'Springboard Sermon': The Point of the Text is Ignored

Closely related is the sermon where the preacher becomes intrigued by something that's a secondary implication of the text, but is not the main point. Imagine a sermon on the wedding at Cana in John 2 that focusses primarily on the lawfulness of Christians drinking alcohol and said nothing about the display of the New Covenant glory of Christ through the sign of Jesus changing water into wine.

One of the great advantages of sequential expository preaching is that the preacher is forced to preach on topics he would rather avoid, and to give appropriate weight to topics he would tend to overemphasise. A preacher of 'unfounded' or 'springboard' sermons can unwittingly jettison both these advantages, and instead God's agenda is silenced or sidelined.

### 3. The 'Doctrinal Sermon': The Richness of the Text Is Ignored

God has deliberately spoken to us 'in many ways' (Heb. 1:1). Too many sermons ignore the literary genre of a passage, and preach narrative, poetry, epistle, and apocalyptic all alike as a series of propositional statements. Whilst all sermons must convey propositional truths, they should not be reduced to them. The literary context of the passages should mean that a sermon from the Song of Songs sounds different than one from Ephesians 5. The passage may have the same central point, but it is conveyed in a different way. The diversity of Scripture is not to be flattened in preaching, but treasured and conveyed in a manner sensitive to the literary genre. Narrative should help us to empathize, poetry should heighten our emotional response, and apocalypse and prophecy should leave us awestruck.

### 4. The 'Shortcut Sermon': The Biblical Text Is Barely Mentioned

The opposite of the exegetical sermon, this kind of preaching shows no exegetical 'working' at all. Though the Lord has set the agenda by His Word, only the preacher is fully aware of that fact. The congregation may well end up saying, 'what a wonderful sermon' rather than 'what a wonderful passage of Scripture.'

Let's keep encouraging our congregation to hear God's voice not just ours, by frequently pointing them back to the text: 'look what God says in verse five' more than 'listen carefully to what I'm saying now.'

## 5. The 'Christ-less Sermon': The Sermon Stops Short of the Saviour

Jesus castigated the Pharisees: 'You study the Scriptures diligently because you think that in them you have eternal life. These are the very Scriptures that testify about me, yet you refuse to come to me to have life' (John 5:39-40). How sad that even we who *have* come to Jesus to have life would bring a whole congregation to study a passage of Scripture and yet refuse to bring them to see what that Scripture says about Christ, turning Old Testament texts into moralistic sermons, and even preaching Christ-less, gospel-less sermons from the Gospels themselves. Imagine the horror of a sermon on Gethsemane narrative that majored on lessons on how we could handle stress in our lives.

If God's Word is like a vast wheel, the hub is Christ and the axle is the gospel. We have not faithfully preached any passage of Scripture until we have worked our way down the spokes to the hub, and communicated what the passage says about Christ and how it relates to the gospel.

# Imposters that Fail to See the Congregation

## 6. The 'Exegetical Sermon': The Text Remains Unapplied

If the 'unfounded sermon' totally misses the text, the 'exegetical sermon' totally misses the congregation. Some preaching that claims to be expositional is rejected as boring and irrelevant ... and rightly so! One could just as well be reading from an exegetical commentary. Everything that is said is true to the passage, but it's not really preaching; it is merely a lecture. Much might be learned about Paul's use of the genitive absolute, but little about the character of God or the nature of the human heart. There is no application to anything but the congregation's minds. True expository preaching will surely first inform the mind, but also warm the heart and constrain the will.

A regular diet of exegetical preaching will make people feel that only topical preaching can be relevant, and will model private Bible reading that presumes we can read God's Word faithfully and remain unchallenged and unchanged.

## 7. The 'Irrelevant Sermon': The Text Is Applied to a Different Congregation

Too much preaching promotes pride in the congregation by throwing bricks over the wall toward other people's greenhouses. Either the point of the passage is applied only to non-believers, suggesting that the Word has nothing to say to the church, or it is applied to problems that are rarely seen in the congregation that is being preached to.

Thus the congregation becomes puffed up, and like the Pharisee in Jesus' parable ends up thankful that they are not like others. The response is not repentance and faith but, 'If only Mrs. Brown heard this sermon!' or 'the local Methodist church really ought to have this sermon preached to them!'

Such preaching will grow the congregation in self-righteousness, not godliness.

### 8. The 'Private Sermon': The Text Is Applied Only to the Preacher

It is easy for the preacher to think merely about how a passage applies to himself, and then to preach to the congregation as if the congregation is entirely in the same situation as the preacher. For me it is certainly easiest to see how a passage of Scripture applies to a white British man in his forties with a wife and six kids who works as a pastor of a small congregation in West London. That may be great for my quiet times, but not much use to my church, as nobody else fits that bill.

What are the implications of the text to the teenager and the single mother? The woman in her forties who'd love to be married and the immigrant? The unemployed and the visiting atheist or Muslim? The congregation as a whole and the bus driver or the office worker or the student or the stay at home mum?

The private sermon can lead to the congregation thinking that the Bible is only relevant to the 'professional' Christian, and that the only valid use of their life would really be to work fulltime for a church or other Christian organization. It can cause the congregation to idolize their pastor and live their Christian lives vicariously through him. It robs the congregation of seeing how to apply the Word to every aspect of their own lives, and how to communicate it to those whose lives are quite different from theirs.

## 9. The 'Hypocritical Sermon': The Text Is Applied to All But the Preacher

The opposite error to the 'private sermon' is the sermon where the preacher is seen as the one who teaches the Word, but does not model what it means to be under the Word.

There are times when a preacher needs to say 'you' and not 'we.' But a preacher who *always* says 'you' and never 'we' does not model how he is only an under-shepherd who is first and foremost one of the sheep who must himself hear his great shepherd's voice, who must know him and follow him, trusting him for his eternal life and security.

A preacher who preaches like this may make the opposite error to the congregation who lives vicariously through their pastor: he will live vicariously through this congregation. He will assume that his discipleship is entirely about his ministry, and end up not walking as a disciple under God's Word at all, but only as one who places others under a Word above which he sits aloof.

### 10. The 'Misfit Sermon': The Point of the Passage Is Misapplied to the Present Congregation

Sometimes the hermeneutical gap between the original passage and the present congregation may be misunderstood, so that the application to the original context is wrongly directly transferred to the present context. So, if the preacher does not have a correct biblical theology of worship, passages about the Old Testament temple might be wrongly applied to the New Testament church building, rather than being fulfilled in Christ and His people. Prosperity gospel preachers might claim the promises of physical blessings given to faithful Old Covenant Israel and flatly apply them to the New Covenant people of God.

## Imposters that Fail to See the Lord

Preaching classes often refer to the two horizons of preaching: the text and the congregation. But the Christian preacher must recognise that behind both stands the Lord who inspired the text and who is at work in the congregation.

### 11. The 'Passionless Sermon': The Point of the Passage Is Spoken, Not Preached

It would be possible to have a preacher who absolutely understood the passage, and spoke about its implications to the congregation present in apt and even profound ways. Yet the preacher delivers the sermon as if he were reading the telephone directory. There is no sense that, as the preacher delivers God's Word, God Himself is communicating with His people. When the preacher fails to recognize that it is God Himself, through His Word, who is pleading, encouraging, rebuking, training, exhorting, moulding, and refining His people through the Spirit's application of that Word, there will often be no passion, no reverence, no solemnity, no evident joy, no sense of sorrow tears—just words.

## 12. The 'Powerless Sermon': The Point of the Passage Is Preached Without Prayer

So much time is given to studying the passage and crafting the sermon, that little time is given to prayer either for correct understanding, or for appropriate application.

The preacher who works hard but prays little trusts much in himself and little in the Lord. It is perhaps one of the biggest temptations to fall into as an expositor, for the more discerning in the congregation will be able to spot false exegesis or inadequate application. But the difference that the prayers of the preacher made to the impact of the sermon will only be clear to the Lord and on the day when all things will be revealed. The horizons of the Lord and of eternity must ultimately be more important to the preacher; in fact, he should only really care about the horizons of the text and the congregation because the horizons of the Lord and of eternity are invisible, yet of infinite importance.

## Conclusion

Expository preaching is so important for the health of the church because it allows the whole counsel of God to be applied to the whole church of God. May the Lord so equip preachers of His Word that His voice may be heard and obeyed.

# ABOUT THE PROCLAMATION TRUST

The Proclamation Trust is all about unashamedly preaching and teaching God's Word the Bible. Our firm conviction is that when God's Word is taught, God's voice is heard, and therefore our entire work is about helping people engage in this life-transforming work.

We have three strands to our ministry:

Firstly we run the Cornhill Training Course which is a three year, part-time course to train people to handle and communicate God's Word rightly.

Secondly we have a wide portfolio of conferences we run to equip, enthuse and energise senior pastors, assistant pastors, students, ministry wives, women in ministry and church members in the work God has called them to. We also run the Evangelical Ministry Assembly each summer in London which is a gathering of over a thousand church leaders from across the UK and from around the world.

Thirdly we produce an array of resources, of which this book in your hand is one, to assist people in preaching, teaching and understanding the Bible.

For more information please go to www.proctrust.org.uk

Get Preaching:

# All-Age Services

Nathan Burley,
Julian Milson & Nigel Styles

ISBN: 978-1-5271-0383-2

## Get Preaching: All-Age Services
Nathan Burley, Julian Milson & Nigel Styles

- Biblical explanation for why all-age services are important
- Practical tips for putting together an all-age service
- Part of the Get Preaching series

The church is an all-age family, and the whole family can grow through hearing the word of God preached. With the Bible at the centre of every service, Nathan Burley, Julian Milson and Nigel Styles give helpful foundations and suggestions for how to include everyone in the church family in the message, before going through a large number of worked examples.

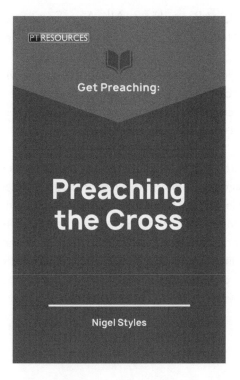

PT RESOURCES

Get Preaching:

# Preaching the Cross

Nigel Styles

ISNB: 978-1-5271-0384-9

## Get Preaching: Preaching the Cross
### Nigel Styles

- Why it is important to preach the cross
- Helpful suggestions for putting it into practise
- Part of the Get Preaching series

The gospel is powerful; we just need to speak it.

In this very practical, short book from the Get Preaching series, Nigel Style reminds us what preaching is, what the message of the cross is, and why that is something to be heralded to all the world. Bringing these two points together he explains the importance of always preaching the cross when preaching the Bible.

AVAILABLE IN THE *TEACHING THE BIBLE* SERIES

PT RESOURCES

TEACHING
JOSHUA

From text to message

DOUG JOHNSON

SERIES EDITORS: JON GEMMELL & DAVID JACKMAN

ISBN 978-1-5271-0335-1

## Teaching Joshua
*From Text to Message*
Doug Johnson

- Text–based study of the book of Joshua
- Part of the 'Teaching' series
- Great for preachers & Bible study leaders

The book of Joshua is an epic. Conquest, battles, scandal, tribalism, deceit, land registration and farewell speeches all make up this remarkable narrative. However behind all the twists and turns, highs and lows is the God who makes and keeps promises. The book of Joshua is profoundly relevant for today and needs to be declared faithfully in its entirety. To be repeatedly reminded through the pages of Joshua that God is faithful to his promises and sovereign over his people, guiding them by his powerful word to his promised rest, is truth we must never tire of hearing.

TEACHING
2 KINGS

From text to message

BOB FYALL

SERIES EDITORS: JON GEMMELL & DAVID JACKMAN

ISBN: 978-1-5271-0157-9

# Teaching 2 Kings
*From Text to Message*
Bob Fyall

2 Kings begins with the succession of Elijah by Elisha and flows largely downward right up to the exile of Judah in Babylon. Amidst the numerous kings and serious failings there are always the vital signs that the true God is still on the throne and working out his purposes in his people and beyond.

Like many other books containing Old Testament narrative, 1 and 2 Kings are both well-known and obscure. Certain stories are very familiar, others seldom preached or taught. It is our hope that this book will greatly help many people dig deeply into this epic narrative and serve people well by teaching it faithfully, relevantly and thoroughly.

Teaching 1 and 2 Kings (of which this is the second volume of two) is an important contribution to our 'Teaching the Bible' series. Bob's guiding hand will be of great assistance to anyone seeking to understand the familiar passages better and explore the lesser known stories well.

# Christian Focus Publications

Our mission statement —

STAYING FAITHFUL

In dependence upon God we seek to impact the world through literature faithful to His infallible Word, the Bible. Our aim is to ensure that the Lord Jesus Christ is presented as the only hope to obtain forgiveness of sin, live a useful life and look forward to heaven with Him.

Our books are published in four imprints:

### CHRISTIAN
## FOCUS

Popular works including biographies, commentaries, basic doctrine and Christian living.

### CHRISTIAN
## HERITAGE

Books representing some of the best material from the rich heritage of the church.

## MENTOR

Books written at a level suitable for Bible College and seminary students, pastors, and other serious readers. The imprint includes commentaries, doctrinal studies, examination of current issues and church history.

## CF4•K

Children's books for quality Bible teaching and for all age groups: Sunday school curriculum, puzzle and activity books; personal and family devotional titles, biographies and inspirational stories — because you are never too young to know Jesus!

Christian Focus Publications Ltd,
Geanies House, Fearn, Ross-shire,
IV20 1TW, Scotland, United Kingdom.
www.christianfocus.com
blog.christianfocus.com